FAMILY WALKS

IN

OXFORDSHIRE

Laurence Main

Scarthin Books, Cromford, Derbyshire 1991

FAMILY WALKS
IN OXFORDSHIRE

Family Walks Series
General Editor: Norman Taylor

———————

THE COUNTRY CODE
Guard against all risk of fire
Fasten all gates
Keep dogs under proper control
Keep to paths across farm land
Avoid damaging fences, hedges and walls
Leave no litter
Safeguard water supplies
Make no unnecessary noise
Protect wildlife, wild plants and trees
Go carefully along country roads
Respect the life of the countryside

———————

Published 1991

Phototypesetting, printing by Nuffield Press Ltd., Cowley, Oxford.

ISBN 0 907758 38 X

TOM TOWER, OXFORD

1

Preface

To take that first, faltering, step over a stile and along a footpath is to turn your back on the artificial world's mad race against time. Even in the citadel of the motor car, footpaths provide escape routes to a more natural, spiritual, world. The ancient paths of Oxfordshire have inspired many, from Arnold to Tolkien. They are a great asset, to be explored and enjoyed by all ages. They can provide great interest, coupled with relaxation and unforced exercise. The routes in this book have been selected to whet the appetites of beginners.

Acknowledgements

I would like to thank the county's Rights of Way Officers for their impressive service. The staff of Oxford's Reference Library were also very helpful. There have been many distant influences. I soon switched from Geography at Westminster College, but not before a field trip had introduced me to the Letcombes (Route 15). I learned to dowse leys at the Rollright Stones (Route 1) on a Dragon Project weekend (organised by 'The Ley Hunter' magazine). Most of all, I must thank my wife, Paule, for testing the walks along with our children, William, David and Chantal, accompanied by their grandmother, Adela Main.

About the author

Laurence Main was born on the approximate site of Roger Bacon's grave (he was used, from infancy, to parties of tourists inspecting the commemorative plaque). When old St Ebbes's was demolished, he learned to appreciate walking in peaceful countryside by taking the towing path of the River Thames from his new home at Donnington to his junior school (South Oxford). Including coming home for lunch, this gave a daily total of five miles walking, from the age of nine. He gained a Bachelor of Education degree from Oxford University and taught in Swindon for six years, later working as Assistant Secretary and Education Officer of the Vegan Society. He is now a full-time writer of footpath guides, including 'The Oxfordshire Trek' (Kittiwake Press), 'King Alfred's Way' (Thornhill Press) and 'Walk Herts & Bucks' (Bartholomew). He also contributes regularly to walking magazines and covers Oxfordshire for 'Out & About'. He now lives in Wales, where he is the voluntary footpaths secretary for the Ramblers' Association in Meirionnydd. He has two other titles in the Family Walks series, covering Mid Wales and Snowdonia.

2

CONTENTS

LOCATION MAP

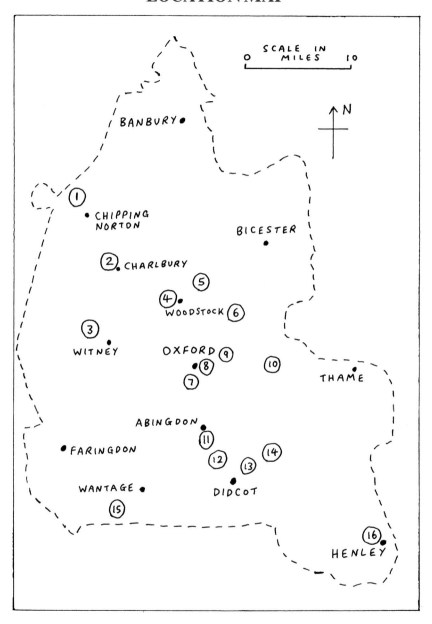

Introduction

This is a book of walks that are especially suitable for families. Hardened backpackers and experienced ramblers are catered for in other books, but here are the relatively short and undemanding walks that will be appreciated by a parent carrying a papoose, or a child with young legs. This may be a woodland walk through a nature reserve, a riverside stroll or a path overlooking watercress beds. The walks also encounter ancient standing stones, an old abbey, a ruined hall and the palace where Sir Winston Churchill was born. Links with famous people abound, although George Orwell hides under his real name of Eric Blair at Sutton Courtenay. Some of the best views of the River Thames can be had from the ancient hillfort at Wittenham Clumps. 'Pooh Sticks' can be bought at nearby Day's Lock to provide entertainment and help the RNLI, but the River Cherwell south of Islip is just as attractive. Swans and cygnets should be seen here, as at Abingdon, while the Oxford Canal forms another wildlife corridor. City-dwellers can take Mesopotamia in their stride—no, it's not in the Middle East but the land between two branches of the River Cherwell in the middle of Oxford. This unique city would take many walks to explore thoroughly, but the main places of interest can be linked by one route. There are plenty of museums for a rainy day!

Oxfordshire is not a large county, although it gained from the county boundary changes of 1974, but it is varied. In the west and north-west are the limestone hills of the Cotswolds, while the chalky Chilterns make the south-east, near Henley, special. The southern border is the prehistoric North Wessex Downs, with the White Horse Uffington overlooking the Vale named after it. The clay of the Thames Valley is crossed by a limestone ridge just south of Oxford, to provide the famous views of the city's 'dreaming spires'. To the north is the Oxfordshire Plain, with Banbury appearing as an outpost of the Midlands.

There is a great sense of history. The underlying rocks are up to 440 million years old and there is evidence of human settlement in the Old Stone Age, 400,000 years ago. Prehistoric men have left plenty to fill the county's museums, while the Romans built Akeman Street and a road which crossed the Thames near their town of Dorchester, but it is the Saxons who have left the lasting impression. Their greatest king, Alfred, was born in Wantage, while Edward the Confessor was baptised in the church at Islip. The Middle Ages brought Oxford University and the wool trade. Charles I made the city his Civil War capital.

5

John Wesley founded Methodism here in the 18th century. William Morris similarly prospered when he built motor cars here in the 20th century.

You won't need a car to enjoy these walks, although a few extra miles may be needed to connect the remoter places, such as the Rollright Stones and Minster Lovell, with a bus service. Oxford is easy to reach by train or coach and at the centre of the county's public transport network. British Rail have even re-opened their line so that you can reach Islip (Route 6) by train. As one who campaigned for the restoration of this service when still at school in the 1960s, I shall feel aggrieved if you don't use it!

The walking season never ends, so don't hang up your boots in the winter, which is often the best season for a short, brisk, walk. Do wear stout shoes and invest in walking boots as soon as you can, however. The practical anorak is not to be eschewed, but jeans are uncomfortable when wet. This is not rugged Snowdonia, but food, drink and spare clothes are best carried in a rucksack. Carry the Ordnance Survey's Pathfinder maps (at a scale of 2½ ins to 1 mile) and practise using them. Children love to use a compass, so why not let them? You may climb Wittenham Clumps this year, but Snowdon next!

THE WHISPERING KNIGHTS

6

MINSTER LOVELL (Route 3)

Symbols used on the route maps

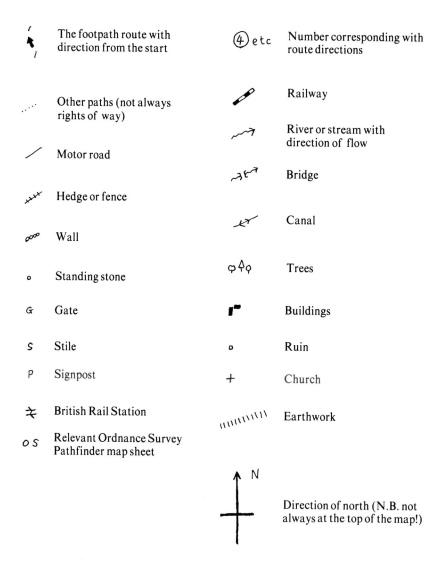

	The footpath route with direction from the start	④ etc	Number corresponding with route directions
	Other paths (not always rights of way)		Railway
	Motor road		River or stream with direction of flow
	Hedge or fence		Bridge
	Wall		Canal
	Standing stone		Trees
G	Gate		Buildings
S	Stile		Ruin
P	Signpost	+	Church
	British Rail Station		Earthwork
O S	Relevant Ordnance Survey Pathfinder map sheet		
			Direction of north (N.B. not always at the top of the map!)

Each map has a scale in miles and a gradient profile showing the height in feet above sea level and the distance in miles from the start.

8

The Rollright Stones

Outline   Lay-by—King's Men Stone Circle—King Stone—Whispering Knights—Brighthill Farm—Lay-by.

Summary   Enigmatic standing stones are the chief reason for coming to this high, windswept, border between Oxfordshire and Warwickshire. The fieldpath below the stones is waymarked and offers fine views.

Attractions   This is one of the most magical places in England and has a splendid old legend attached to it. A king and his army were conquering England when they reached Rollright, where they were confronted by a witch. She challenged the king thus:

'Seven strides thou shalt take
And if Long Compton thou canst see
King of England thou shalt be.'

The king proceeded, crying:

'Stick, stock, stone
As King of England I shall be known!'

A mound, known as the arch-druid's barrow, blocked his view however. The old witch mocked him, saying:

'As Long Compton thou canst not see
King of England thou shalt not be.
Rise up, stick, and stand still, stone,
For King of England thou shalt be none.
Thou and thy men hoar stones shall be
And I myself an eldern tree.'

If the King's Men were turned into the 76 stones of the circle, it must have happened around 2000 BC, while the Whispering Knights (famous for a humming sound at full moon) may be older. The King Stone is eight feet tall and across the road (part of the ancient Jurassic Way) in Warwickshire. Fairies live in a nearby hole and dance around it at night. There really is an underground bunker nearby, but staffed now and again by members of the Royal Observer Corps. A fascinating, detailed, account of the Dragon Project's work here, involving ultrasound, radiation, a photograph of an aura around the King Stone at dawn and much more is contained in Paul Devereux's book 'Places of Power' (Blandford, 1990). Alfred Watkins (of 'Old Straight Track' fame) reckoned the old tale was a reference to a ley running from Long Compton church through the King Stone to Chipping

continued on page 12

9

Route 1

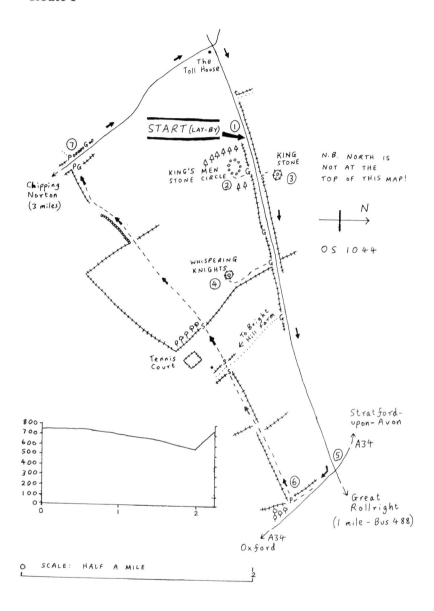

The Toll House

START (LAY-BY) ①

⑦ PG GND
PG

Chipping Norton (3 miles)

KING'S MEN STONE CIRCLE ②

KING STONE ③

WHISPERING KNIGHTS ④

N.B. NORTH IS NOT AT THE TOP OF THIS MAP!

N

OS 1044

Tennis Court

To Bright Hill Farm

Stratford-upon-Avon

↑ A34

⑤

⑥

Great Rollright (1 mile - Bus 488)

← A34 Oxford

SCALE: HALF A MILE

Route 1

The Rollright Stones   2¼ miles

START: *The stones are three miles north-west of Chipping Norton, beside a minor road going west of the A34. The King's Men and the King Stone can be seen from the road and there are convenient lay-bys. The monuments are privately owned. Admission, for which there is a small charge, is during daylight hours (G.R. SP 295309).*

ROUTE

1. *Go from the lay-by to the stone circle, which is visible nearby.*
2. *Cross the road and go over a stile to see the King Stone.*
3. *Return over the stile and turn left along the road until the second gate on your right. Turn right through this to follow the path to the Whispering Knights.*
4. *Return to the road and go right, resuming your former direction. Continue to the junction with the A34.*
5. *Turn right along the verge of the A34, towards Oxford. After 200 yards, climb to a waymark post.*
6. *Go ahead, as waymarked, with a hedge on your left. Continue with the hedge on your right in the next field. Cross a farm access track and pass a tennis court on your left to reach a stile just to the right of a line of trees ahead. Go over it and maintain your direction across a field. Walk with a wall on your left for a while and descend to a road.*
7. *Turn right uphill to a crossroads. Turn right to pass The Toll House and return to the lay-by near the stone circle.*

Public Transport   Be prepared for some extra road walking! The Midland Red bus No. 488 between Banbury (where there is a British Rail station) and Chipping Norton stops in Great Rollright, just over one mile to the east of route direction 5. (In the event of making this approach, you would, of course, start the circuit here by turning left along the A34 towards Oxford, having reached the crossroads from the opposite direction to people walking from point 4.) Telephone Banbury 262368 for details of this bus service. You can reach Chipping Norton (from where it is three miles along a minor road via Over Norton and Choicehill Farm to the Rollright Stones, passing point 7) by bus from Oxford (Oxford Minibus Nos. 20, 20A, 20B and 20C).

11

Norton church and castle. Another ley goes in the direction of Madmarston Hill camp (SP 386389).

Refreshments Stock up in Chipping Norton!

WEST OF CHARLBURY

Route 2   4½ miles

West of Charlbury

Outline   Charlbury Station—Walcot Farm—Catsham Lane—River Evenlode—Charlbury Station.

Summary   The Oxfordshire Way can't make up its mind which route to take west of Charlbury, so it splits. This walk follows both branches. A good track forms the route south of the River Evenlode, while fieldpaths provide a contrast on the northern, return, route.

Attractions   Time seems to stand still on this walk through harmonious countryside. Walcot Farm belonged to John de Langelee in 1302. Its high eaves are unusual in Cotswold farmhouses. The fine track which passes close to it forms part of the Oxfordshire Way. This 65 mile trail goes from Bourton-on-the-Water (which happens to be in Gloucestershire) to Henley-on-Thames. It thus links the Cotswolds with the Chilterns, two Areas of Outstanding Natural Beauty. Originally conceived by the CPRE (Council for the Protection of Rural England) it is now waymarked and maintained by Oxfordshire County Council. The River Evenlode leads to Charlbury, the Saxon 'town of freemen'. St Diuma, first Bishop of the Mercians, was buried in St Mary's church upon his death in 658. A small museum in Market Street is open on Sundays (2–4 p.m.) from April to October. There is a small charge for adults (children enter for free).

Refreshments   There is a choice of places in Charlbury.

YELLOWHAMMER yellow and brown 16cm

13

Route 2

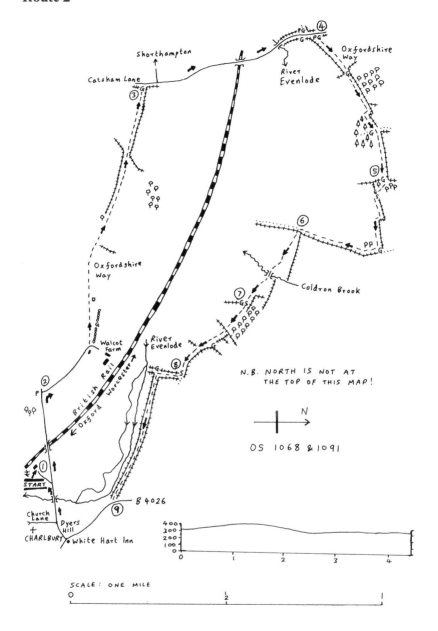

Shorthampton

Catsham Lane

③

Oxfordshire Way

River Evenlode

④

Oxfordshire Way

⑤

⑥

Coldron Brook

⑦ GS

Oxfordshire Way

Walcot Farm

River Evenlode

British Rail

Oxford Worcester

②

P

⑧

N.B. NORTH IS NOT AT THE TOP OF THIS MAP!

N

OS 1068 & 1091

①

START

Church Lane

CHARLBURY

Dyers Hill

White Hart Inn

⑨

B 4026

400
300
200
100
0

0   1   2   3   4

SCALE: ONE MILE

0   ½   1

14

Route 2

West of Charlbury   4½ miles

START: *Charlbury Station is best reached by train. It is just off the B4437 on the western side of Charlbury, from which it is separated by the River Evenlode. Charlbury is 17 minutes by train from Oxford (G.R. SP 352195).*

ROUTE

1. *Go to the main road and turn left, crossing a bridge over the railway.*

2. *Turn right along a No Through Road, signposted 'Oxfordshire Way'. Pass Walcot Farm on your right and follow the track between wheat fields.*

3. *Turn right along Catsham Lane. Ignore the road to Shorthampton on your left and descend to cross the railway and the river.*

4. *Turn right through a gate to follow the signpost 'Oxfordshire Way'. Walk with a hedge on your right, then on your left in the next field.*

5. *Take the waymarked gate in the corner and bear right. Continue over a stile beside a small gate in the hedge opposite. Turn left along the headland path, turning right with it at a corner.*

6. *Look for a yellow waymark arrow on your left and cross, as indicated, into a corner of a field. Walk beside a hedge on your left, then veer slightly right to a footbridge over Coldron Brook. Go ahead with a hedge on your left, then follow a fence on your left, as waymarked.*

7. *Cross a stile to the left of a gate to follow a waymarked path past a copse on your left. Go ahead over waymarked wooden bars to walk with a hedge on your left. Continue to the corner of the next field.*

8. *Cross a stile and bear right along an old green lane, following it round a left-hand bend.*

9. *Reach the B4026 and turn right into Charlbury. Turn right at the White Hart Inn down Dyers Hill. Church Lane is on your left, while the station is ahead, across the bridge over the Evenlode and on your left.*

Public Transport   Charlbury is on British Rail's Oxford–Worcester line.

THE DOVECOTE, MINSTER LOVELL

16

Route 3   3½ miles
Minster Lovell

Outline Minster Lovell Church—Crawley—River Windrush—Minster Lovell Hall—Minster Lovell Church.

Summary The tranquil valley of the Windrush provides a relaxing walk which finishes at interesting ruins now in the care of English Heritage. (There is an admission fee to visit the hall, but the path back to the church is a right of way.)

Attractions The peaceful setting hides a tragedy. When the foundations for a new chimney were being laid in Minster Lovell Hall in 1708, the workmen discovered a secret underground room. Breaking in, they found a man's skeleton seated at a table upon which was a book, pen and paper. All quickly turned to dust, but it was believed that a great mystery had been solved. Francis Bacon had commented on it in his 'History of Henry VII' (1622) reporting that Lord Lovell had escaped from defeat at the Battle of Stoke, near Newark, in 1487, and survived for a long time in a vault. Francis, the ninth Baron Lovell, had supported the Yorkist Richard III, who created him Viscount Lovell in 1483. As Constable of Wallingford Castle, Chamberlain of the Household and Chief Butler of England, he was a powerful man, as the old doggerel verse stated:

'The catte, the ratte and Lovell the dogge
Ruleth all England under the Hogge'.

Two other favourites of the king were the catte (Catesby) and the ratte (Ratcliffe), while the dogge referred to Lovell's crest. The Hogge was King Richard, whose crest included a wild boar. This unpopular ruler was soon to lose his life and crown at the Battle of Bosworth in 1485. Francis Lovell fled to Flanders and missed the news that the Wars of the Roses were now officially over and Henry VII had founded the new Tudor dynasty. He returned to support the rebellion of the pretender, Lambert Simnel. After fleeing from his defeat, it would seem that the servant who would have kept him supplied with food and drink in his refuge died, leaving his master to perish of hunger and thirst. Henry VII, who had granted Lovell's estate to Jasper Tudor, visited the hall in 1494. Perhaps he ate some pigeons from the dovecote.

The village was originally called Minster and took this name from the church (a 'monasterium'). This is dedicated to St Kenelm, a young king of Mercia murdered by his ambitious sister in 822. This dedication was chosen by William, the seventh Baron Lovell, when he rebuilt the church in the

continued on page 20

17

Route 3

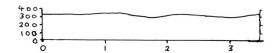

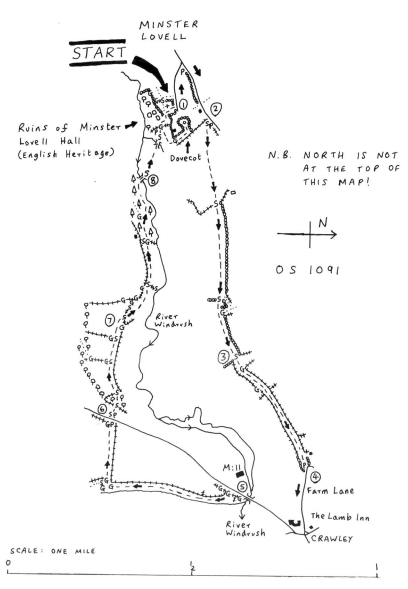

MINSTER LOVELL

START

Ruins of Minster Lovell Hall (English Heritage)

Dovecot

N.B. NORTH IS NOT AT THE TOP OF THIS MAP!

N

OS 1091

River Windrush

Mill

Farm Lane

The Lamb Inn

CRAWLEY

River Windrush

SCALE: ONE MILE

0   ½   1

18

Route 3
Minster Lovell 3½ miles

START: *Minster Lovell is just north of the B4047 two miles west of Witney. The church is in a cul-de-sac with room for a few cars to park. There is a larger car park at the sports ground near the bridge. The Hall and Dovecot are open daily, 10 a.m.–6 p.m., April–September and Tuesdays–Sundays, 10 a.m.–4 p.m., October–March (G.R. SP 324114).*

ROUTE

1. *Walk back up the access lane from the church and turn right, away from the village.*

2. *Bear right over a stile to follow the signposted path across a field to another stile. Go ahead over it and follow a wall on your left to a third stile, ignoring a track bearing left in the corner. Continue over the stile to a fourth (without a step) in the next corner.*

3. *Cross the stile and go ahead to a hedged lane. Follow this to a road.*

4. *Turn right to the crossroads in Crawley, where you turn right, then fork right. Cross a bridge over the River Windrush.*

5. *Take the second gate on your left after the bridge and follow a path between a stream on your left and a hedge on your right. Go ahead through a gate and turn right immediately to go through another gate and walk uphill beside a hedge on your right to the road again.*

6. *Cross the stile on the opposite side of the road to follow the signposted path across the narrow field to woodland. Bear left down through the trees and cross a stile in the bottom left corner. Walk with a ditch and a fence on your right through two fields.*

7. *In the third field, turn right over a stile and immediately turn left to walk with a hedge on your left. Enter woodland and bear right at a fork to descend to a footbridge over the river.*

8. *Having crossed the footbridge, bear left up to the ruins of Minster Lovell Hall. Before entering them, however, follow a path on your right around to the Dovecot.*

9. *Return from the Dovecot to the Hall and bear right to the church.*

Public Transport You'll have to walk from Witney! The shortest way would be to follow two miles of road to Crawley and start there. Buses run to Witney from Oxford (Oxford Minibus Nos. 11 and 100).

1430s. The earlier church was dedicated to St John. South of the village, across the Witney road and on the hilltop, are the Charterville Allotments. This was a practical application of a Land Settlement Scheme by Feargus O'Connor, who was recognized as the 'champion of popular rights' when elected MP for County Cork in the election after the great Reform Act of 1832. Too extreme for the Chartists, Feargus raised nearly £11,000 to buy 300 acres here and build houses. He induced families to move to them and become self-sufficient off a few acres of land attached to each. This also qualified them to vote, when the franchise was restricted to owners of freehold property with a minimum annual value of 40s (£2). The scheme failed but the well-built houses remain. Nearer the church is The Street, whose picturesque Cotswold cottages are now highly valued. They used to be rented out at 6d (2½p) a year. The money wasn't worth taking the trouble to collect, so the tenants lived rent free. Every eleventh year, however, they had to vacate the properties, with all their belongings, for one day, in order not to acquire squatter's rights.

Refreshments The Olde Swan, Minster Lovell and The Lamb Inn, Crawley.

WOODSTOCK

20

Route 4   3¼ miles

Blenheim Park

Outline   The Stocks, Woodstock—Chaucer's Lane—Blenheim Park—
Column of Victory—Fair Rosamund's Well—Column of Victory—
Woodstock.

Summary   This walk would fit in well with a visit to Blenheim Palace. This
most splendid of stately homes can be seen across the lake, while the Column
of Victory and Fair Rosamund's Well are passed by this route. This is classic
parkland, created by Lancelot 'Capability' Brown in the 18th century. Easy
tracks and grassland add to the enjoyment of this walk.

Attractions   This walk starts from the Oxfordshire County Museum in
Fletcher's House, Park Street, Woodstock. As well as the permanent
galleries, there are temporary exhibitions. Admission is free and this
museum is open daily, 10 a.m.–5 p.m. (10 a.m.–6 p.m. Saturdays, 2–6 p.m.
Sundays), May–September and Tuesdays–Sundays, 10 a.m.–4 p.m. (10
a.m.–5 p.m. Saturdays, 2–5 p.m. Sundays), October–April. Outside are the
stocks. These have survived as a reminder of the administration of justice
and the punishment of offenders in the not too distant past. We may find
them amusing, but those who had to endure them in the 19th century found
them far from entertaining. It is only recently that the idea of punishment for
crime has moved away from gratuitous cruelty. The stocks were reserved for
lesser offences—the serious cases swung on the local gibbet. This did save a
lot of money, avoiding the need for prisons. The stocks were designed to
secure the prisoner's legs (I don't know why there are five holes in the ones at
Woodstock). The weather had to be endured, as well as the sentence, which
could range from a few hours to several days. Spectators would gather to
ridicule the prisoner, perhaps emptying their chamber pots over his head.
There may be more to stocks than meets the eye. The dowser Guy
Underwood, in his fascinating book 'Pattern of the Past' (1969), recorded
how water lines formed the symbol of protection and mercy at stocks. This
would have affected the nervous system of the culprit, bringing a sense of
dejection and gloom. It seems that our ancestors knew precisely where
everything should be located.

Going up Park Street, visitors to Blenheim Palace should go through
the Triumphal Arch, just beyond where this route turns right along
Chaucer's Lane. The palace is normally open daily, 11 a.m.–6 p.m., mid-
March–October. The home of the Duke of Marlborough and the birthplace
of Sir Winston Churchill, it is one of England's most stately homes. The site
of the old royal manor house which, together with nearly 1800 acres of

continued on page 24

21

Route 4

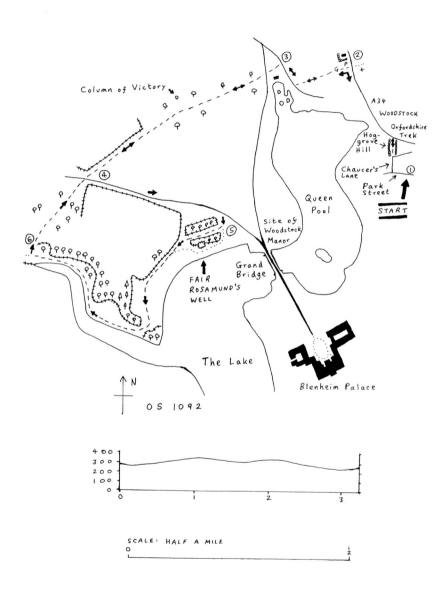

Column of Victory

Queen Pool

A34
WOODSTOCK
Oxfordshire
Trek

Hog-
grove
Hill

Chaucer's
Lane

Park
Street

START

Site of
Woodstock
Manor

FAIR
ROSAMUND'S
WELL

Grand
Bridge

The Lake

N

OS 1092

Blenheim Palace

SCALE: HALF A MILE

22

Route 4
Blenheim Park   **3¼ miles**

START: *Woodstock is eight miles north of Oxford on the A34. Cars can be parked for free in Park Street, near the Oxfordshire County Museum, where this walk starts (G.R. SP 444168).*

ROUTE

1. *With your back to the museum, go right along Park Street and turn right at Chaucer's Lane. Go down steps to the A34, turn left and walk beside it until your reach a small derelict church on your right.*

2. *Turn left and go through a gate giving access to Blenheim Park. Go ahead to reach an estate road near a corner of a lake. Turn right along this for 100 yards.*

3. *Turn left across the grass just beyond a house, cross a second road and maintain your direction uphill, passing close to the Column of Victory on your right. Follow a wire fence on your right to a road ahead.*

4. *Turn left along the road for nearly half a mile.*

5. *Just before the Grand Bridge, bear right along the right of way. Walk with the lake on your left to the tip of its western arm.*

6. *Turn right to walk up a valley and back to the road. Go ahead across it to retrace your steps past the Column of Victory, now on your left, and out of the park, where your turn right back to Woodstock.*

Public Transport   Woodstock can be reached by bus from Oxford (Oxford Minibus Nos. 20, 20A, 20B and 20C). Between 1890 and 1954 you could have arrived by train along a line financed by the Duke of Marlborough.

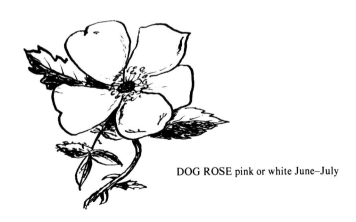

DOG ROSE pink or white June–July

parkland were conferred on John Churchill, the first Duke of Marlborough, in 1705, by Queen Anne, in gratitude for his defeating the French, lies near point 5 of this route. Henry II used to visit his mistress Fair Roz, Rosamund Clifford, here in the 12th century. His jealous queen, Eleanor, had her murdered, but her name lives on in the holy well nearby.

The Column of Victory is also passed on this route. This was finished in 1730 at a cost of £3000. It is 134 feet high, with a lead statue of the first duke at the top.

Refreshments Woodstock has a choice of places offering refreshments, which can also be obtained in Blenheim Palace.

ON THE OXFORD CANAL

Rock of Gibraltar

Outline   Rock of Gibraltar Inn—Oxford Canal—Pigeon Lock—Lince Lane—Rock of Gibraltar Inn.

Summary   A gentle stroll beside the canal leads to Pigeon Lock. This is where the Oxfordshire Trek turns across the bridge over the canal towards Bletchingdon. We follow it as far as Lince Lane, where a right turn along this road completes the circuit. The canal shares the valley of the River Cherwell, along which the railway was also to come. The 'navvies' took their refreshment at the Rock of Gibraltar Inn, from where boat trips can be arranged (tel. 0993 881339).

Attractions   The Rock of Gibraltar has stood firm for over two hundred years, exuding character and history. The name probably comes from the visit of General Eliott to Oxford, to receive the freedom of the city, in 1787. He had heroically resisted attacks on the Rock, of which he was Governor, by both France and Spain. It is possible that he came this way while extending his visit to Blenheim Palace. The same general is commemorated in a pub name at South Hinksey (Route 7). The pub was built in 1787 by proprietors of the Oxford Canal. This waterway had just reached Enslow, where a new wharf opened that September to sell coal at 13 pence a cwt. The Industrial Revolution had arrived in this corner of rural Oxfordshire and made it, temporarily, the southern terminus of the Oxford Canal, dug to bring coal from the Midlands to the university city. It finally reached Oxford and the River Thames (for access to London) in 1790. The Grand Junction Canal (now the Grand Union) was to open a decade later, however, and successfully competed against it. Now the Oxford Canal is popular with pleasure craft and the Rock is famous amongst canal enthusiasts. They must make a change from its earliest customers, who would have been the rough 'navvies' digging the canal, the boatmen, local quarry workers and farm labourers, then railway workers in the mid 19th century. A station on the Oxford–Banbury line was built near the Rock but it is, unfortunately, closed now. Day-trippers started to come here from Oxford in the 1860s and 1870s when Enslow aroused national interest. The thigh bones of a very big dinosaur, the Cetiosaurus oxoniensis, were discovered by workmen in one of the local quarries. They can now be seen in the University Museum, Oxford (Route 8). Today, ramblers following the Oxfordshire Trek, the 64 mile long distance route around Oxford, pass this way.

Refreshments   The Rock of Gibraltar Inn, Enslow.

Route 5

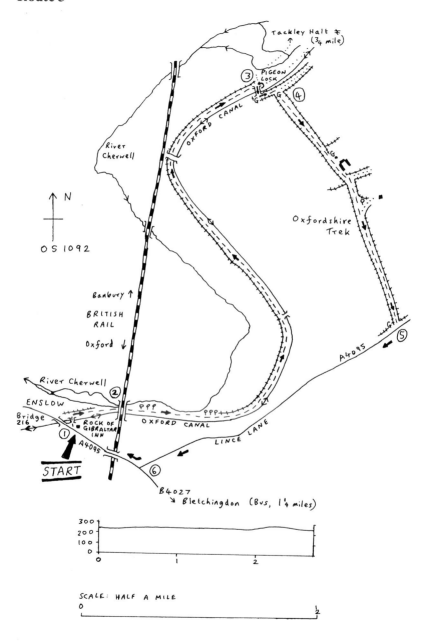

Tackley Halt ⚶
(¾ mile)

③ PIGEON LOCK

④

River Cherwell

N

OS 1092

Oxfordshire Trek

Banbury ↑
BRITISH RAIL
Oxford ↓

A4095

⑤

River Cherwell
ENSLOW
Bridge 216
ROCK OF GIBRALTAR INN
① A4095
② OXFORD CANAL
LINCE LANE

START

⑥

B4027
↘ Bletchingdon (Bus, 1¼ miles)

300
200
100
0
0   1   2

SCALE: HALF A MILE
0   ½

26

Route 5
Rock of Gibraltar 2¾ miles

START: *The Rock of Gibraltar is beside Bridge 216 across the Oxford Canal on the A4095 between Woodstock and Bletchingdon (G.R. SP 482182).*

ROUTE

1. *Cross the old canal bridge and turn right along the towing path to walk with the canal on your right.*

2. *Continue under the bridge carrying the main railway line between Oxford and Birmingham. Follow the canal towing path for another mile, passing a draw bridge on your right and going under another bridge.*

3. *Reach Pigeon Lock and cross the bridge over the canal here. Turn left along a track for 20 yards to another track on your right.*

4. *Turn right at this junction and follow the track away from the canal. Continue past Vicarage Farm on your left to reach a road (Lince Lane).*

5. *Turn right along Lince Lane to reach the B4027. Go right to cross the bridge over the railway and reach the Rock of Gibraltar Inn on your right.*

Public Transport   In the old days there were canal water-buses called 'fly boats'. Now you have to walk from the nearest railway halt or bus stop. The easiest would be to bus to Bletchingdon (service Nos. 25 and 25A between Oxford and Bicester, run by Oxford Minibus) and walk one and a half miles each way along the B4027. If you have the guide book to the Oxfordshire Trek, you could follow the footpath route from Bletchingdon to Lince Lane (one mile each way) and start this route at point 5. You could also follow the Oxfordshire Trek from Woodstock (three miles each way to the Rock of Gibraltar Inn from the bus stop for Oxford Minibus Nos. 20, 20A, 20B and 20C between Oxford and Chipping Norton). If you prefer rail travel, some trains still stop at Tackley Halt, nearly a mile by footpath north of Pigeon Lock (point 3). In this case, take the Ordnance Survey Pathfinder Map Sheet 1069 (Bicester), as well as Sheet 1092 for Enslow, and start at G.R. SP 485205.

ST. CHRISTOPHER, WOODEATON CHURCH

Route 6

4¾ miles

South of Islip

Outline Islip—Oxfordshire Trek—River Cherwell—Woodeaton—
Oxfordshire Way—Islip.

Summary Short sections of two long distance paths are joined by a bit of
road walking. The Oxfordshire Trek takes well-defined fieldpaths to a
delightful riverside walk beside the Cherwell. It then heads along a track to
Woodeaton, with its magnificent little church. The Oxfordshire Way is
joined near Noke and provides a contrast. The land is higher and there are
fine views over Otmoor and the valley of the Ray.

Attractions Islip is a well-kept secret, being one of the most beautiful
villages in Oxfordshire. Walkers know this, of course, because two long
distance paths converge on it. It has the attraction of two rivers, the Ray and
the Cherwell, whose confluence is at the south-western end of the village. St
Nicholas's church has an impressive tower, befitting the place where
Edward the Confessor was baptised in 1004. He was born in a palace built by
Ethelred the Unready which stood just to the north of the village. Edward
was crowned in 1043 as our last Saxon king before Harold (who died at the
Battle of Hastings). His lasting achievement was the construction of
Westminster Abbey, which was given the manor of Islip. The connection was
sealed when John of Islip became Prior of Westminster in 1500. Simon of
Islip had earlier become Archbishop of Canterbury, in 1348. The bridge over
the River Ray saw action in the Civil War. Essex led his Roundheads in an
attack on it on 17th June, 1643, but was repulsed. He returned in triumph on
28th May, 1644. Royalist cavalry under the Earl of Northampton were back
in the village the next April, but were routed by Cromwell himself on 23rd
April, 1645. In more peaceful times, Islip was a busy stage on the coach route
between London and Worcester, once boasting 21 inns. Woodeaton seems to
be a place that history has passed by. Its Church of the Holy Rood is a little
gem, containing a 14th century wall painting of St Christopher carrying the
Christ child. This faces the door to make it easier for travellers to see it. An
inscription reads: 'Look upon this image and verily on this day you shall not
die an evil death.' There is a doom inscription on a rood beam, a manorial
pew, a minstrel's gallery and a 13th century tower built inside the church.

Refreshments Islip has the Red Lion, the Swan Inn and shops.

Route 6

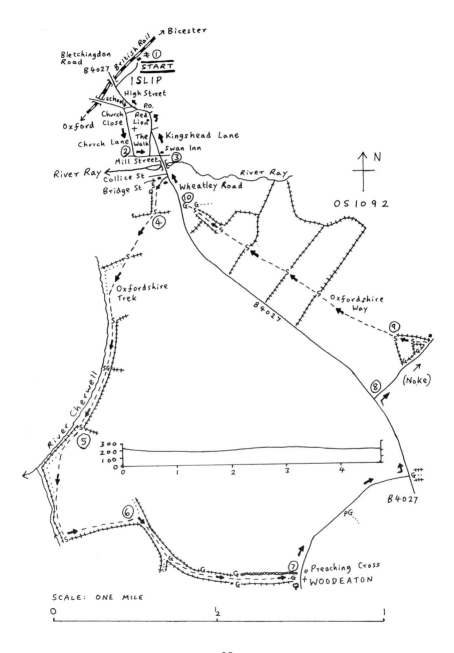

Route 6

South of Islip   4¾ miles

START: *Islip can, once again, be reached by train, on the Oxford–Bicester line. Please use this service. There's even a new station for you. If you must drive, park near the Red Lion in the centre of Islip, which is halfway between Oxford and Bicester on the B4027 one mile south of the A43 (G.R. SP 526144).*

ROUTE

1. *Go up the access lane from the British Rail station to reach the Bletchingdon Road and turn left towards Islip. Veer right at the war memorial and go ahead up Church Close. Pass the church on your left and continue down Church Lane.*

2. *Turn left along Mill Street. Pass The Walk on your left and reach the Swan Inn.*

3. *Turn right over the bridge across the River Ray. Pass Collice Street on your right but bear right immediately up Bridge Street. Do not cross a stile ahead, but bear left past allotments to a stile in the next corner.*

4. *Cross the stile and bear right across a field. Continue across another stile and bear right to the River Cherwell. Turn left to walk beside the river on your right. Go ahead over a stile to walk between a hedge on your left and the river. Continue over a stile beside a gate, pass an old boathouse and cross another stile ahead.*

5. *Emerge in the corner of a field. Walk around it with a hedge on your right and the field on your left. Ignore a stile in the second corner (the right of way has been diverted) and continue to join a track in the third corner.*

6. *Turn right to follow the track to the road opposite Woodeaton church.*

7. *Go left up the road past a medieval preaching cross on your right. Reach the B4027 and turn left along its verge for a quarter of a mile.*

8. *Take the lane on your right towards Noke. Pass a 'Caution Children' sign and a gate on your left, then turn left up a narrow, hedged path waymarked as the Oxfordshire Way.*

9. *Go ahead along the waymarked Way back to the road.*

10. *Go right back to Islip, taking Kingshead Lane towards the station.*

Public Transport   Islip is on British Rail's Oxford–Bicester line.

THE REED BEDS

Route 7   2¾ miles
Happy Valley

Outline   South Hinksey—Happy Valley—Chilswell Copse—South Hinksey.

Summary   There is some climbing on this walk, but not really strenuous. Fieldpaths lead to Happy Valley and its nature reserve. A delightful woodland path leads across the stream and to a board walk through reedbeds.

Attractions   South Hinksey is an attractive village unfortunately too close to the A34. It also seems to be too close to the city for its church doors to remain unlocked. You can, at least, inspect the base of a 15th century preaching cross in the churchyard of St Laurence's which is, curiously, spelt differently to St Lawrence Road. Hengist, the Saxon leader who arrived with Horsa in the fifth century, may have given his name to Hinksey. It is certainly at the foot of the old Arthurian frontier between Saxons and Celts. (Read S. G. Wildman 'The Blackhorse Men'.) The welcoming pub is named the General Eliott after the hero of the Rock of Gibraltar (see Route 5). The noisey A34 is only to be expected, of course, for Matthew Arnold observed that 'in the two Hinkseys nothing keeps the same'. Refrain from dropping bombs on the speeding cars and lorries as you cross the bridge over it. Instead, admire the view over the 'dreaming spires of Oxford'. It's all peace and tranquility when you do reach Happy Valley. Also known as Chilswell Valley, there is a helpful notice along the path which tells you all about its natural history. This is a 'deeply incised gorge' with reedbeds at its easterly end, deciduous woodland in the middle and 'calcareous grassland being invaded by scrub in the west'. Practically all the other reedbeds in Oxfordshire have been 'improved' by drainage. Reed bunting, sedge warbler and reed warbler are three of the birds based here. Blue tits, stock dove and tawny owl find homes in the woodland, which is mostly oak and ash with a hazel understorey. There are plenty of nuts for squirrels and small rodents. Come in April and May to see the bluebells. The grassland is a splendid spot for a picnic. Wild liquorice, wild thyme, rockrose, cowslip, common spotted and bee orchids can be seen here in the summer. Look in the sky for kestrels, while there is a large colony of marbled white butterflies in July. The summer also brings huge numbers of meadow browns, hedge browns and common blues. Blackcap and whitethroat nest in the encroaching blackthorn scrub.

Refreshment   The General Elliot, South Hinksey.

33

Route 7

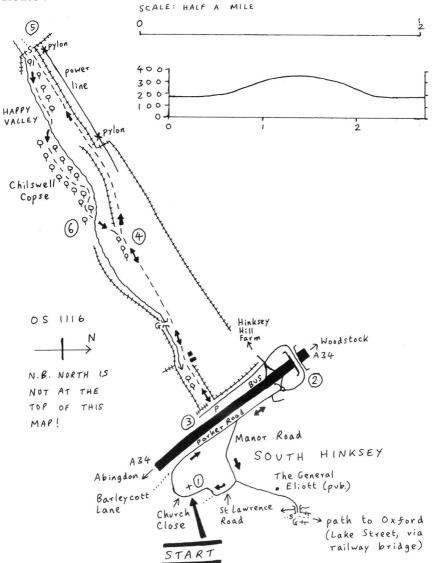

SCALE: HALF A MILE

0   ½

⑤

S Pylon

power line

Q

HAPPY VALLEY

Q

Pylon

Chilswell Copse

Q

⑥   ④

400
300
200
100
0

0   1   2

OS 1116

→ N

N.B. NORTH IS NOT AT THE TOP OF THIS MAP!

Hinksey Hill Farm

Woodstock A34

BUS

②

③   P

Parker Road

Manor Road

SOUTH HINKSEY

A34

Abingdon

Barleycott Lane

Church Close

①   St Lawrence Road

The General Eliott (pub.)

S
G

→ path to Oxford (Lake Street, via railway bridge)

START

34

Route 7
Happy Valley
2¾ miles

START: *The church of St Laurence is the focal point of South Hinksey, but motorists should note that the landlord at The General Eliott is obliging when it comes to parking space. Access by road is off the A34 south-west of Oxford. The best approach, however, is by foot from Oxford. Lake Street leads off the Abingdon Road to Hinksey Swimming Pool (open air), near which is a boating lake. Go left at the end of Lake Street, away from the swimming pool, and turn right to cross the big lake, created when gravel was extracted to build the railway in 1844, by a long footbridge. This leads to Jacob's Ladder, the steps up the bridge across the railway and the former site of marshalling yards (for car-transporters from Cowley). A metalled and enclosed path leads on the other side to South Hinksey—just half a mile from the swimming-pool but like a world away (G.R. SP 510040).*

ROUTE

1. *Go right from the church to follow Church Close to Parker Road. Continue along this towards the bridge over the A34, on your left.*

2. *Cross the Bridge over the A34 and follow the signposted Chilswell Path, ignoring a private drive to Hinksey Hill Farm on your right.*

3. *Leave the metalled lane by turning right, as signposted, along a track which goes past some houses on your right. Ignore a bridge on your left and go ahead up a fieldpath parallel to power lines on your right.*

4. *Ignore the board walk through the reedbeds on your left. Go ahead with a hedge at first on your left, then on your right. Reach a stile in a corner near a pylon on the other side of the hedge.*

5. *Do not cross the stile. Turn sharply left along a path which crosses the stream and goes through woodland.*

6. *Bear left along the board walk across the reedbed and return to your outward path. Retrace your steps to the start.*

Public Transport There is an extremely infrequent bus service to a stop near the bridge over the A34 (Oxford Bus Nos. 44 and 45 from Oxford to Boar's Hill). The short walk from Oxford is recommended.

A FAMILY WALK (Route 6)

Route 8 4¼ miles

Oxford

Outline Tourist Information Centre—Alice's Shop—Christ Church Meadow—Merton Street—Bridge of Sighs—Radcliffe Camera—St Michaels's—University Museum—Keble College—Ashmolean Museum—Worcester College—Oxford Castle—Covered Market—Tourist Information Centre.

Summary These four miles may take you several days. Don't worry about the pavement pounding. Here are delightful meadow paths, cobbled roads and interesting alleys.

Attractions The Tourist Information Centre is in St Aldate's, a corruption of 'Old Gate'. It only acquired this name in 1774, after the fishmongers who did business here moved into the new covered market. The Town Hall, opposite the TIC, was opened by the future Edward VII in 1897. On its corner with Blue Boar Street is the Museum of Oxford (open Tuesdays–Saturdays, 10 a.m.–5 p.m., free admission). Walking south brings Christ Church College on your left, with Christopher Wren's Tom Tower. This houses a great bell called Tom which weighs 18,000 lb and came from Osney Abbey. It rings 101 times at 9.05 p.m. (9 p.m. on the Oxford meridian) which is when the original 101 students had to be in by. Oxford's patron saint, Frideswide, built a monastery for monks and nuns here in 727 and her shrine is in the cathedral which the 'House', as the college is known, can boast as its chapel. Fourteen students have gone on to become Prime Ministers in England's other 'House'. Cardinal Wolsey founded the college in 1525, intending to name it after himself. Changing times led to his ambition being thwarted. A maths lecturer here in the late 19th century became famous for his children's books. Lewis Carroll was the pen-name of the Rev. Charles Dodgson. Alice was the daughter of the Dean of Christ Church (that is the college principal). Dodgson used to buy her sweets in what is now called Alice's Shop. The lady who ran it is pictured as a sheep in 'Through the Looking Glass'.

Point 2 takes you into Christ Church Meadow, crossing the culverted Trill Mill Stream, once explored by T. E. Lawrence (of Arabia) when he was a student at Jesus College. Be near Point 3 in May to see 'The Eights' when crews from each college row in bumping races. Just past Point 4 is a plaque commemorating the first English balloon trip. This was made by James Sadler from near this spot on 4th October, 1784. He landed near Woodeaton (Route 6). Dead Man's Walk was the route taken by coffins being carried to

continued on page 40

Route 8

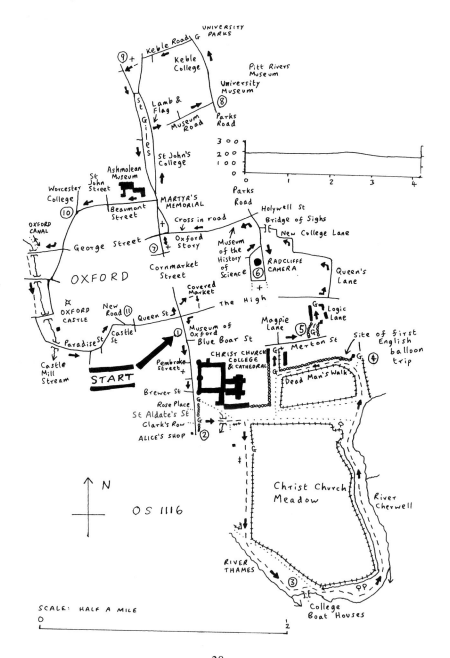

Route 8
Oxford   4¼ miles

START: *Oxford's Tourist Information Centre is at the top of St Aldate's, near Carfax, the centre of the city (G.R. SP 514061).*

ROUTE

1. *Go right from the Tourist Information Centre along St. Aldate's Street to Alice's Shop on your right.*

2. *Cross the road from Alice's Shop to go through the gate into the War Memorial Gardens and Christ Church Meadow. Turn right to the River Thames. Go left to walk with the river on your right.*

3. *Follow the path with the River Cherwell on your right to the gate for Rose Lane, near the Botanic Gardens, but do not go through it.*

4. *Go left along Dead Man's Walk and turn right through the gate in the next corner to reach Merton Street. Go right along its cobble stones.*

5. *Turn left along Logic Lane to The High. Cross this carefully to go ahead up Queen's Lane. Turn left at Catte Street to walk between the Radcliffe Camera and the University Church of St Mary the Virgin (whose tower gives the best views in Oxford).*

6. *Return up Catte Street and turn left along Broad Street. When you reach Cornmarket Street go left to St Michael's church.*

7. *Go right to retrace your steps past Broad Street and inspect the Martyr's Memorial before going up the right hand side of St Giles past St John's College to the Lamb and Flag, where you turn right along a passage to Museum Road. Go ahead to the University Museum.*

8. *Facing the museum, go left to Keble College and turn left along Keble Road, then ahead to St Giles' church.*

9. *Turn left down the other side of St Giles and turn right along Beaumont Street, passing the Ashmolean Museum.*

10. *Go left along Worcester Street. Turn right along Hythe Bridge Street and take the riverside path on your left. Go ahead along this and Paradise Street, passing Oxford Castle on your left. Go up Castle Street to Bonn Square, near Westgate Shopping Centre.*

11. *Go along Queen Street (renamed from Butcher Row in 1788 in honour of George III's queen, Charlotte). Go left at Carfax, whose 14th century tower is all that remains of St Martin's church, to Cornmarket Street. Go through the Golden Cross Shopping Arcade to the Covered Market. Return to Carfax by way of the High and go left back to the start.*

Public Transport Trains and coaches to Oxford.

the old Jewish Cemetery whose site is now occupied by the Botanic Gardens (Route 9). It may also have been where Royalist Colonel Windebank was shot for treason in 1645.

Merton Street still has its 18th century cobble stones. Merton College is the college with the oldest statute, being officially founded in 1274. Its Mob Quad was built between 1304 and 1378, while its library claims to be the oldest in England. Point 5 leads to Logic Lane and University College, which some claim to date from 872, when King Alfred the Great reputedly founded it. Its official foundation was in 1280.

Cross The High to Queen's Lane. The queen was Edward III's Philippa whose chaplain founded Queen's College for 'poor boys' from the north of England. George II's queen, Caroline, has her statue under the cupola of the college, however. Dinner is traditionally announced here with a trumpet and the Boar's Head ceremony is maintained at Christmas. New College is virtually unchanged since 1400 and the city wall is preserved in its garden. The Bridge of Sighs (a copy of the bridge in Venice) links Hertford College's north and south quadrangles. The Radcliffe Camera (Point 6) was the first round library in England in 1749. It is now a reading room of the nearby Bodleian Library, a legal deposit library with nearly five million books in subterranean storage areas. The public can view exhibitions (which could include the manuscript of Kenneth Grahame's 'The Wind in the Willows') on weekdays, 9 a.m.–5 p.m. (12.30 p.m. Saturdays). The Sheldonian Theatre was built by Wren in 1669 and houses degree ceremonies. Next door is the Museum of the History of Science (open weekdays 10 a.m.–1 p.m. and 2.30–4 p.m.). Between the Oxford Story (open daily from 9 a.m.) and Balliol College (founded in 1282 as a punishment on John de Balliol for kidnapping the Bishop of Durham) is a cross in the middle of Broad Street. This marks the spot where the Protestant martyrs, Bishops Latimer and Ridley in 1555 and Archbishop Cranmer in 1556 were burnt outside the city walls. St Michael's church (Point 7) has a tower dating from 1050 and a sheila-na-gig (Celtic fertility image). Pass the Martyr's Memorial (erected in 1841) to St Giles', where Charles I's troops were drilled during the Civil War. The Univeristy Museum is open weekdays 12–5 p.m., while the Pitt Rivers Museum is open weekdays 1–4.30 p.m. In the chapel of Keble College hangs the famous picture 'The Light of the World' by the pre-Raphaelite painter William Holman Hunt. Guy Fawkes' lantern is on display in the Ashmolean Museum (open 10 a.m.–4 p.m. weekdays, 2–4 p.m. Sundays). Just before Point 10, at 24 Beaumont Street, is the birthplace of Richard the Lionheart (1157).

Refreshments   Plenty of choice in Oxford.

Mesopotamia

Outline University Parks—Mesopotamia—Marston Road—Angel Meadow—Magdalen Bridge—Botanic Gardens—Longwall Street—University Parks.

Summary This walk illustrates how easy it is to follow paths through peaceful countryside yet stay within the centre of Oxford.

Attractions May is the best month to visit the University Parks, for you should find Oxford University Cricket Club playing first class opponents. The home side has fielded talent such as Colin Cowdrey, the Nawab of Pataudi and Imran Khan in the past. You can watch the cricket free, although a collection is taken and charges collected for seats. The two arms of the River Cherwell make Mesopotamia, where the path is attractively lined by willow trees. Returning along the road, notice the church of St. Clement. This was built in 1828 as a replacement for the old church demolished at The Plain. Before reaching this, sample Greyhound and Angel Meadows, from where the tower of Magdalen College makes a fine picture. Pass the massive red Florey Building, which was completed (to house students) in 1971 and reach The Plain. This channels three main roads from the east on to Magdalen Bridge. The roundabout is the churchyard of old St. Clement's. A plaque on one of the lamp-posts surrounding it proclaims the false peace of 1814, before Napoleon escaped from Elba. There has been a bridge here since the 11th century, but Magdalen College (pronounced Maudlin) was built in the 15th century. Visit it to see the deer park and cross a bridge to spot a Snakeshead Fritillary in Magdalen Meadow (it blooms in late April and early May). Choristers welcome in the summer at dawn on May Morning at the top of Magdalen tower. Below lies the Botanic Gardens, founded in 1621 as the Physic Garden to exhibit the whole range of flowering plants in the world. The yellow Oxford Ragwort (from Mount Etna) escaped from here to colonise southern England. Open 8.30 a.m.–5 p.m. weekdays, 10 a.m.–12 p.m. and 2 p.m.–6 p.m. on Sundays. The greenhouses, where bananas can be seen growing in winter, are open daily 2 p.m.–4 p.m. As you return past St. Cross church, look beyond its churchyard to an adjacent cemetery. Kenneth Graham, the author of 'The Wind in the Willows' and Alastair, the son for whom he wrote the book, are both buried here. Look for a Celtic cross commemorating Sir John Stainer, the composer and Professor of Music. Also buried here is Kenneth Tynan, the theatre critic. Between the church and Holywell's 16th century manor is

continued on page 44

41

Route 9

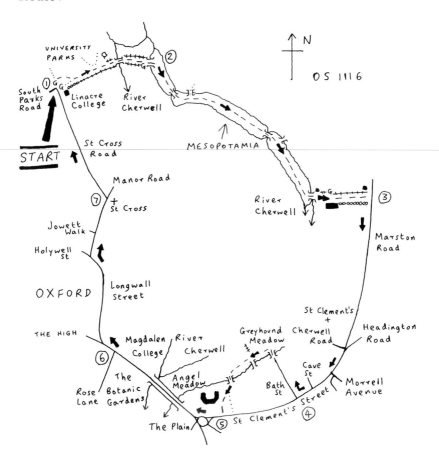

UNIVERSITY
PARKS

②

N
OS 1116

South
Parks
Road

① G
Linacre
College

River
Cherwell

MESOPOTAMIA

START

St Cross
Road

Manor Road

⑦ ✝ St Cross

River
Cherwell

③

Jowett
Walk

Holywell
St

OXFORD

Longwall
Street

Marston
Road

THE HIGH

Magdalen
College

River
Cherwell

St Clement's
✝
Cherwell
Road

Headington
Road

⑥

The
Botanic
Gardens

Rose
Lane

Angel
Meadow

Greyhound
Meadow

Cave
St

Bath
St

Morrell
Avenue

The Plain

⑤ St Clement's Street

④

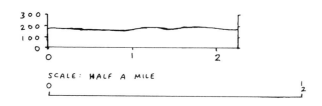

300
200
100
0

0   1   2

SCALE: HALF A MILE
0   1/2

Route 9
Mesopotamia

2¼ miles

START: *At the corner of South Parks Road and St Cross Road is an entrance to the University Parks. There is no public right of way here, but the gates are usually open in daylight hours (G.R. SP 518070).*

ROUTE

1. *Enter the University Parks and turn right to walk with a fence on your right to a path which leads over two bridges across the two arms of the River Cherwell.*

2. *Bear right along the concrete track between the two arms of the river. Ignore two footbridges on your left, then follow the path across the third footbridge and go ahead to Marston Road.*

3. *Turn right along the pavement of Marston Road, passing St Clement's church on your right. Pass Cherwell Road and Cave Street on your right.*

4. *Turn right down Bath Street and take the footbridge to Greyhound Meadow. Turn left to enter Angel Meadow (the names come from two old pubs), ignoring another footbridge immediately on your left. Take the next footbridge across the River Cherwell on your left to pass the red Florey building on your right.*

5. *Turn right along St Clement's Street to The Plain and go ahead across Magdalen Bridge, which overlooks the playing fields of Magdalen College School on your left. Visit the Botanic Gardens on your left and Magdalen College on your right. Resume your former direction to pass Rose Lane on your left.*

6. *Turn right up Longwall Street, walking beneath the 15th century battlements of Magdalen College's long wall on your right. The deer park is on the other side of it. Bear right at a fork to follow St Cross Road, passing the church on your right.*

7. *Ignore Manor Road on your right. Bear left up St Cross Road, between sports grounds, to return to the start.*

Public Transport Trains and coaches to Oxford.

a chapel over the site of the holy well. This was built in 1862 by the Clewer Sisterhood, who reclaimed 'fallen women' for respectable domestic service. The well dried up after drainage operations around 1800 lowered the water table.

Refreshments   There is a choice of places in Oxford.

THE OLD LOCK-UP, WHEATLEY

Wheatley

Outline   Wheatley—Shotover House—Wheatley.

Summary   Starting from an interesting village, cross parkland to a firm track which leads past Shotover House. A steady climb to a lane brings the reward of an easy return to Wheatley.

Attractions   Wheatley's rowdy past is testified to by the old 'Lock-up'. It dates from 1834 when there were still highwaymen and stage coaches using the Oxford–London road. The Sun Inn is another survivor of that era. The cock-fighting and bull-baiting pit is gone. The formal layout of an 18th century park survives at Shotover House. Sir Timothy Tyrrell, the Ranger of Shotover Forest, had enclosed the first park and built the first house here in the mid 17th century. Sir James Tyrrell transformed this in the early 18th century by digging a long canal where there had been fishponds and building a new house. A little Gothic temple closed the vista at the far end of the long canal, making it an early example of a Gothic folly. William Kent was the probable architect of this building. His own drawings for it have recently been discovered and sold to the U.S.A. It is a perfect specimen being large, gabled, battlemented, pinnacled, turreted, mysterious, enigmatic and old.

Refreshments   Wheatley has the Sun Inn and shops.

THE SUN INN

45

Route 10

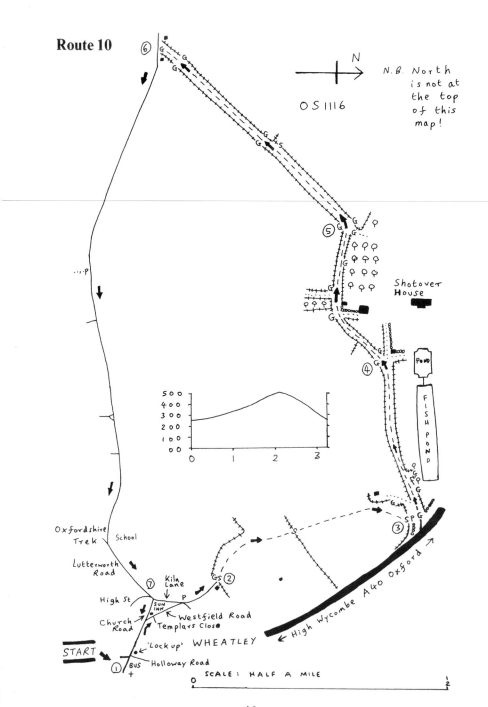

N

OS 1116

N.B. North is not at the top of this map!

Shotover House

PoND

FISH POND

500
400
300
200
100
00

0   1   2   3

⑥

⑤

④

③

②

①

⑦

Oxfordshire Trek

School

Lutterworth Road

High St

Kiln Lane

P

GS

SUN INN

Church Road

Westfield Road

Templars Close

'Lock up' WHEATLEY

START

BUS

Holloway Road

High Wycombe A40 to Oxford

SCALE: HALF A MILE

0   ½

Route 10
Wheatley

3¼ miles

START: *Wheatley lies just south of the A40, the main road between Oxford and London, three miles east of Oxford. This walk starts from the bus stops near the church of St Mary the Virgin, which was completed in 1868 by the distinguished Victorian architect George Edmund Street at the instigation of Samuel Wilberforce, Bishop of Oxford (G.R. SP 596058).*

ROUTE

1. *Go right from the church (left from the bus shelter) to pass the old 'Lock-up' on your right, just after the crossroads. Continue up Church Road to the Sun Inn and bear right along Westfield Road. Ignore Templars Close on your right. Go ahead at a crossroads and reach a stile beside a gate giving access to a field.*

2. *Cross the stile and cross the field to another stile in the fence ahead. Go over this and veer right towards the far right corner of this field, with the A40 on your right.*

3. *Cross a signposted stile and turn left, away from the A40. Ignore a track forking left almost immediately. Go ahead along the fenced drive, passing the ornamental lake on the site of the old fish ponds on your right. Shotover House can be seen ahead, on your right.*

4. *Bear left at a track junction, away from Shotover House. Climb past side tracks on your right and your left to walk with woodland on your right.*

5. *Turn left with the track to follow a wide avenue all the way to a lane.*

6. *Turn left along the lane downhill to Wheatley, passing a school on your left. Go ahead along the Lutterworth Road to pass the High Street on your right and fork right, away from Kiln Lane on your left. This brings you back to the Sun Inn, on your left. Retrace your steps along Church Road to the start.*

Public Transport Trains used to run to Wheatley from Oxford and Princes Risborough, but Dr Beeching took his scalpel to most of that route in the 1960s. The little bit that remains is only for freight traffic from Cowley (and there's not much of that now). Fortunately, there is a good bus service to Wheatley from Oxford and Aylesbury (Service No. 280).

CULHAM CUT

South of Abingdon

Outline   Abingdon—River Thames—Culham Cut—Swift Ditch—Causeway—Abingdon.

Summary   This is a peaceful riverside stroll from a town that used to be the capital of Berkshire. The return along a short section of the A415 is made bearable by the elevated causeway for pedestrians.

Attractions   Abingdon grew up around an abbey that was the sixth richest in England at the Dissolution in 1538. Its foundation has been dated to the late seventh century, but little now remains. What has been discovered beneath the Abbey Grounds indicates that the church must have been splendid. A gate survives next to St Nicholas' church, while the old exchequer buildings can also be seen. Abingdon Museum houses relics of the abbey. Located in the Old County Hall, this is open Tuesdays–Saturdays, 1–5 p.m. (small admission fee). The Hall is a reminder of the town's former status, which was lost in 1867 to Reading. Abingdon later became part of Oxfordshire, in 1974. The town brought this decline upon itself when it refused to allow the Great Western Railway to build its main line between London and Oxford through it. Reading, of course, became the G.W.R.'s great junction, while Abingon had to wait until 1873 for a branch line (from Radley). Closed to passenger services in the 1960s, this was kept open for freight, principally MG cars. When their production ceased in 1980, the track's days were numbered. The final train ran in 1984, taking passengers to a place that had already lost its station. The Old County Hall befitted the capital of Berkshire, being designed by Christopher Kemster, a pupil of Wren. Completed in 1682, its cupola bears comparison with the one on top of the Sheldonian Theatre in Oxford. It is an Abingdon tradition to throw buns from the roof of the hall on special royal occassions. Another reminder of the town's function as a capital is the County Gaol, built by Napoleonic prisoners of war between 1805 and 1811. It spent nearly a century from 1874 as a store for a corn merchant before its present incarnation as an attractive arts and leisure centre. The Tourist Information Centre is housed within this. On the way back to Abingdon from Culham this route follows the old road across a fine 15th century stone bridge. This was built by the Brotherhood of the Holy Cross, a guild of Abingdon merchants. It spans Swift Ditch, which was the original course of the River Thames, before the monks of Abingdon Abbey dug the channel that now flows between Abingdon's Abbey Grounds and Abbey Meadow. The bridge that now

continued on page 52

49

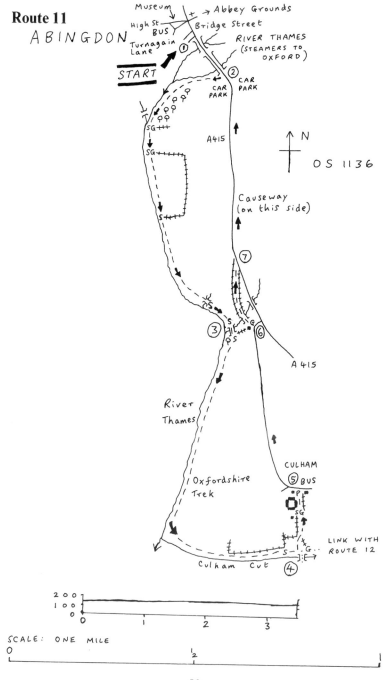

Route 11

ABINGDON

Museum → Abbey Grounds

High St. ┼ Bridge Street

BUS

Turnagain Lane ① RIVER THAMES (STEAMERS TO OXFORD)

START ②

CAR PARK

CAR PARK

SG +++

SG +

A415

↑ N

OS 1136

S +++

Causeway (on this side)

⑦

S ⑥
G
③
S
S

A 415

River Thames

CULHAM

⑤ BUS

Oxfordshire Trek

SG

LINK WITH ROUTE 12

S — I. G.

Culham Cut ④

200
100
0

0 — 1 — 2 — 3

SCALE: ONE MILE

0 — ½ — 1

Route 11

South of Abingdon   3½ miles

START: *Abingdon's Tourist Information Centre is in the Old Gaol, just off Bridge Street (G.R. SP 295309).*

ROUTE

1. *Go right to cross the bridge over the two branches of the River Thames and an island formed by them (and from where Salter's steamers depart for Oxford).*

2. *Turn right to walk along the towing path beside the River Thames on your right. Notice the classic view of Abingdon, with the spire of St Helen's church rising above 18th century almshouses on the opposite bank, near where an iron bridge marks the confluence of the River Ock with the Thames. The Old Gaol's distinctive shape is another landmark. Go ahead over two stiles beside gates, then over a third stile to walk past open meadow. A little footbridge is followed by a stile and, at a corner of a bend in the river, another stile leads to a more substantial footbridge.*

3. *Cross this and continue with the River Thames on your right until the path bends left to follow the Culham Cut. This channel was cut to improve navigation when the river was the main highway. After walking along an enclosed path, cross a stile to see a bridge ahead.*

4. *Do not cross the bridge or continue along the towing path, unless you wish to link this walk with Route 12 here. This route continues by turning left, away from Culham Cut. Walk with a hedge on your right at first, then go through a gap to put it on your left. Go ahead to the road near the bus stop in Culham.*

5. *Turn left along this minor road, until it bends right towards the A415.*

6. *Bear left at the bend in the road to take a gate and follow the old road over the old bridge, built between 1416 and 1422. Follow the old road to its junction with the A415.*

7. *Cross the A415 carefully and turn left along the Causeway to walk back to Abingdon.*

Public Transport   There are plenty of buses to Abingdon. Oxford Minibus run services 30, 30A, 31, 32 and 32A from Oxford, while Oxford Bus Co. run services 42, 43, 44, 45 and 302 from Oxford. Oxford Tube service 390 runs from Oxford to London via Abingdon (and Henley). If you are walking in the summer, why not travel in one direction between Oxford and Abingdon by steamer along the River Thames? Contact Salter Bros. Ltd., Folly Bridge, Oxford, tel. (0865) 243421.

carries the A415 over Swift Ditch was built in 1928. The Brotherhood of the Holy Cross also built the Causeway that runs beside the A415. This provided medieval travellers with a dry route.

Refreshments   There is a choice of places offering refreshments in Abingdon.

ALL SAINTS CHURCH

Sutton Courtenay

Outline   Culham Lock—All Saints' Church, Sutton Courtenay—The Abbey—Sutton Pools—Culham Cut—Culham Lock.

Summary   The River Thames is seen in a variety of poses, from canal to lake, but it is especially attractive just north of Sutton Courtenay. There is a serene atmosphere to the walk around the village, with plenty of famous graves to locate in the churchyard.

Attractions   Sutton was a royal residence visited by William the Conqueror and Henry I, whose first child was born here. It acquired the rest of its name when it was granted to Reginald de Curtenai in 1161. The Abbey was built in the 14th century as a summer residence for the Abbot of Abingdon. Spend time in the churchyard to find the tomb of Herbert Henry Asquith (1852-1928). As the last Liberal Prime Minister (from 1908 to 1916) he is buried directly behind the church. The novelist George Orwell is buried in a typically modest way near the far right hand corner as you stand with your back to the back of the church. He also hides under his real name of Eric Blair (1903-1950). Elsewhere is the grave of Mrs Martha Pye, who died in 1822 aged 117. Sutton Pools is an inspiring backwater created by the digging of Culham Cut in 1809. Before that, the mill over the river charged extortionate fees for opening the weir (because of the inconvenience to the miller).

Refreshments   George & Dragon, Sutton Courtenay.

MEADOWSWEET cream June–Sept.

Route 12

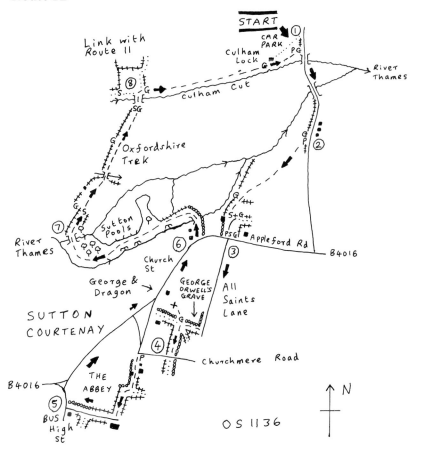

START

CAR PARK

① PG

Culham Lock

River Thames

Link with Route 11

⑧ S G

culham Cut

SG

G Oxfordshire Trek

G P ②

G S ⑦

Sutton Pools

River Thames

G

S+G

P S G Appleford Rd

B4016

⑥

Church St

③

George & Dragon

GEORGE ORWELL'S GRAVE

All Saints Lane

SUTTON COURTENAY

G

④

Churchmere Road

B4016

THE ABBEY

⑤

BUS

High St

↑ N

OS 1136

200
100
0

0   1   2

SCALE: HALF A MILE

0   1/2

54

Route 12

Sutton Courtenay   2¼ miles

START: *Motorists should start from the car park at Culham Lock. This can be reached by a minor road going south from the A415 two miles south of Abingdon (G.R. SU 508949).*

ROUTE

1. *Go right from the car park to follow the road across two bridges over the Culham Cut and the River Thames. Continue past houses on your left.*

2. *Go through a gate on your right and follow the signposted footpath. This leads to the far corner of the field, where there is a way out to Appleford Road (the B4016).*

3. *Cross the road carefully to follow All Saints Lane ahead. This bends right after passing tne churchyard wall, then left opposite the side entrance to the churchyard.*

4. *Turn right along Churchmere Road, then turn left along the signposted track at the next corner to walk with the grounds of The Abbey on your right. (Various courses are held here, including those of the Gandhi Foundation. The Dalai Lama is a recent distinguished visitor.) Go right when you come to a T junction with a lane.*

5. *Emerge in Sutton Courtenay's High Street, near the bus stops. THIS IS WHERE YOU COULD START THE WALK IF YOU COME BY PUBLIC TRANSPORT. Go right to a triangular junction and bear right to walk past the church and the George and Dragon pub on your right.*

6. *Bear left along the path in the corner formed by Church Street and Appleford Road. Follow the footpath beside the river and across the weirs.*

7. *Veer right to cross the stile and follow the well-defined path over a small footbridge into the next field. Continue with a fence on your left to the bridge ahead. Cross it to reach the linking point with Route 11.*

8. *Turn right to complete this route by following the towing path of Culham Cut, on your right, back to Culham Lock.*

Public Transport   You could bus to Culham by Oxford Tube's No. 390 service (from Oxford to London via Abingdon and Henley). This stops at The Lion, about a quarter of a mile from Culham Lock. Buses Nos. 32, 32A and 302 serve Sutton Courtenay at The Triangle (Point 5) and link the village with Oxford and Didcot, where there are British Rail stations. Alternatively, you could link this walk with Route 11.

BESIDE THE CHERWELL (Route 6)

Wittenham Clumps

Outline Car Park—Castle Hill—Day's Lock—Little Wittenham Wood —Castle Hill—Car Park.

Summary Climb the Wittenham Clumps for a fine view up the Thames Valley, then descend to Day's Lock to buy 'Pooh Sticks' (two for a penny). Return across Church Meadow and through Little Wittenham Wood to Castle Hill. Descend from this hillfort back to the car park.

Attractions Nearly all of this walk is within Little Wittenham Nature Reserve. This and the superb views, both up the Thames Valley and across the Vale of White Horse to the Ridgeway, would be enough to make this a special walk. There is much more, however—an otherworldly atmosphere summed up by the rumour of a spectral raven that guards a treasure. It is in a ditch, known as the Money Pit, on the eastern side of Castle Hill. Castle Hill is a place of great significance. Dowsers have shown that there are male (Michael) and female (Mary) energy lines coiled around the famous ley or dragon line which extends from St Michael's Mount in Cornwall to Bury St Edmunds in Norfolk by way of Glastonbury Tor and Avebury. This ley crosses the Thames at nearby Clifton Hampden, where St Michael's church is built on a mound. The male (Michael) energy line curves through the ring of trees on top of Castle Hill, however. Within this sacred grove is a node or crossing-point with the female (Mary) line coming from Dorchester Abbey. More on this subject can be found in John Michell's 'The New View Over Atlantis' (1983) and 'The Sun and the Serpent' by Hamish Miller and Paul Broadhurst (1989). Look for a poem carved on the easterly tree of the clump. It dates from the 1840s:

> 'As up the hill with labouring steps we tread.
> Where the twin clumps their sheltering branches spread,
> The summit gained, at ease reclining stay,
> And all around the wide-spread scene survey....
> Where the low banks the country wide surround
> The ancient earthwork formed old Mercia's bound....
> While at our feet where stands that stately tower
> In days gone by up rose Roman power.
> And yonder there, where Thames' smooth waters glide,
> In later days appeared monastic pride.
> Within that field where lies the grazing herd
> High Walls were crumbled, stone coffins disinterred.

continued on page 60

Route 13

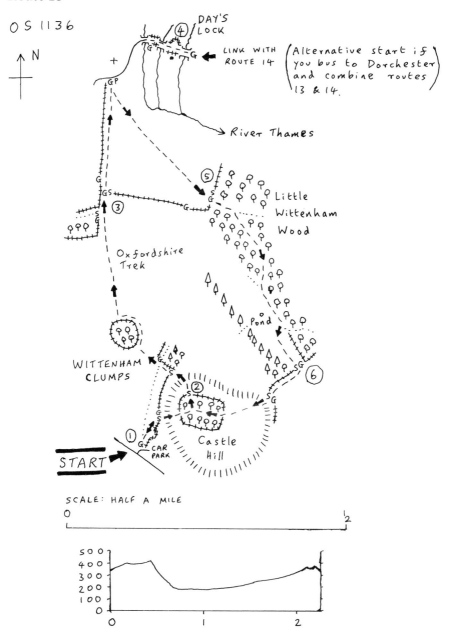

OS 1136

N

DAY'S LOCK
④

G — G   LINK WITH ROUTE 14

(Alternative start if you bus to Dorchester and combine routes 13 & 14.)

GP

→ River Thames

⑤   Little Wittenham Wood

G
GS
③   G

Oxfordshire Trek

Pond

WITTENHAM CLUMPS

⑤ G S

②   ⑥

G   SG

START →   ①   G   CAR PARK

Castle Hill

SCALE: HALF A MILE

0   2

500
400
300
200
100
0

0   1   2

Route 13

Wittenham Clumps $2\frac{1}{4}$ miles

START: *Motorists should start from the car park at the foot of Castle Hill, on its southern side. This is on a minor road one mile north-west of the A4130 at Brightwell-cum-Sotwell (G.R. SU 567924).*

ROUTE

1. *Go up the hill from the car park, bearing right over a stile beside a gate to reach the earthworks of Castle Hill. Enter the sacred grove of trees and bear left at a path junction to reach a stile.*

2. *Cross the stile and go ahead down to another stile at the foot of the castle ditch. Walk with a fence on your right and across a track to the second clump of trees, on Round Hill. Go right around the perimeter fence of the young trees, planted to replace the old beeches. Look for Day's Lock in the Thames Valley below you and descend in its direction to a stile beside a gate in the bottom corner of the field. Ignore another stile beside a gate on your left just before it.*

3. *Descend beside the hedge on your left to a road. Go right to Day's Lock, with its 'Pooh Sticks'. LINK WITH ROUTE 14 HERE.*

4. *Retrace your steps to the nature reserve. On entering it, bear left to cross the meadow diagonally to a stile beside a gate giving access to woodland.*

5. *Follow the woodland path to a fork and bear right. Reach a clearing and go left. When this path returns to the woodland on your left, go right up to a stile in the top corner.*

6. *Cross the stile and turn right to follow the hedge on your right up to a stile next to a gate. Go over this to enter the hillfort again and follow the path back to the sacred grove of trees. Reach the path junction and bear left to retrace your steps to the car park.*

Public Transport The nearest bus stop is in Dorchester, so link with Route 14 at Day's Lock. The two routes give a combined total of $4\frac{3}{4}$ miles.

Such, in the course of time, is the wreck which fate
And awful doom award the earthly great'.

Refreshments   See link with Route 14.

THE GEORGE HOTEL, DORCHESTER

Route 14   2½ miles

Dorchester

Outline   Dorchester Abbey—Dyke Hills—Day's Lock—Dorchester Abbey.

Summary   History is all around you as the path leads from a medieval abbey across the site of a Roman town to Iron Age earthworks. A walk beside the Isis leads to its confluence with the Thame.

Attractions   The ancients knew how to recognise magical spots. This is one, being the real start of England's most famous river. What we now call the Thames from Kemble through Oxford to here is really the Isis. Once upon a time names really meant something and dreamy old Oxford has a vague memory of this, still calling its stretch of river the Isis. Dorchester on Thames is really Dorchester on Thame. The River Thame flows past it to join the Isis and thereby create the Thames (Thame–Isis). This transformation occurs in a remarkably pretty spot, marked by the attractive Day's Lock. A flash lock and weir have existed here since 1580. This was fine going downstream, but barges needed to be winched upstream. The present pound lock was installed in 1788/9. It was quite costly at £1,078, so tolls were levied at 4d per ton. By 1793 they were reduced to 2½d. A large settlement existed here during the Iron Age, as witnessed by the Dyke Hills. Perhaps this was a trading centre, being on the border of three tribal territories. The Dobunni occupied the Upper Thames Valley and the Cotswolds, while to their east, in the Chilterns, were the Catuvellauni and to their south, in the Middle Thames Valley and on the chalk downs, were the Atrebates. Dorchester must have been an important trading centre under the Romans too, with a tax office here. Its rich inhabitants in the fourth century AD hired Saxon mercenaries ('foederati'). Perhaps this is why, unlike other Roman towns, it seems that the Saxons took the place over in the fifth century AD and became town-dwellers themselves. Christianity was probably not new to the town when St. Birinus came as a missionary from Pope Honorius I in 635 and received a royal grant of land in Dorchester for the establishment of an episcopal see and a cathedral church. When the strong authority of the Normans took control, Oxford and Wallingford were assuming regional importance and Dorchester was in decline. The former cathedral became an abbey in 1140. One of its glories was the Jesse Window, showing the ancestry of Jesus. Sir Richard Beauforest bought the abbey church at the Dissolution, for £140, then gave it to the parish. The old monastery guest house became a school and is now a museum, with free

continued on page 64

61

Route 14

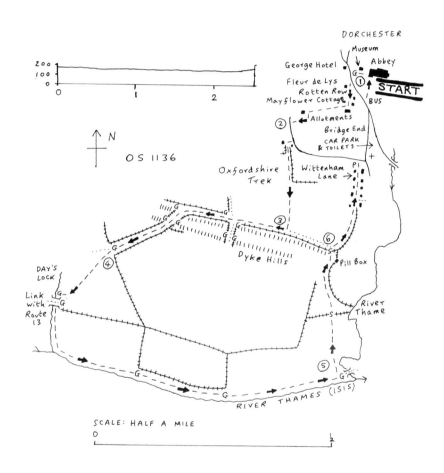

200
100
0

0   1   2

↑ N

OS 1136

DORCHESTER

Museum
George Hotel
Abbey
Ⓖ
Fleur de Lys
①
START
Rotten Row
Mayflower Cottage
BUS

②
Allotments

Bridge End
CAR PARK
& TOILETS →

Oxfordshire
Trek
Wittenham
Lane
P

③

⑥

Dyke Hills
Pill Box
DAY'S
LOCK
④
Ⓖ

Link
with
Route
13
Ⓖ
River
Thame

⑤

SCALE: HALF A MILE
0   ½

RIVER THAMES (ISIS)

Route 14
Dorchester   2½ miles

START: *Dorchester Abbey is in the centre of Dorchester, which is now by-passed by the A423 nine miles south-east of Oxford (G.R. SU 579942).*

ROUTE

1. *Go right from the porch of the Abbey to pass the medieval preaching cross and the museum. Go through the gate to the road and turn left. Cross carefully to the Fleur de Lys Inn (dating from 1530) and go up Rotten Row. Turn right past Mayflower Cottage and follow the path over the allotments (the site of the Roman town) to a lane.*

2. *Go left along the lane for 100 yards, then take the signposted path on your right, beginning between houses and continuing with a fence on your left. Go ahead across a field to the ancient earthworks of the Dyke Hills.*

3. *Turn right to walk with the Dyke Hills on your left. Go ahead over a private track and along a fenced path. Bear left with this.*

4. *Cut across a meadow to Day's Lock. Do not cross the footbridge over the river unless you wish to link with route 13 here. This route continues by going along the riverbank under the bridge and following the Isis, to give the river its proper name, as far as a footbridge over the Thame near the confluence.*

5. *Having resisted the impulse to cross the footbridge, turn left to walk back to the Dyke Hills, crossing stiles in fences.*

6. *Go ahead to enter Dorchester along Wittenham Lane. Keep straight on past the Roman Catholic church in Bridge End, near the car park. Cross the road near the bus stops to enter the grounds of the abbey.*

Public Transport   Oxford Bus Co. share their service No. 5 with Bee Line. This links Dorchester with Oxford and Reading. There is also Oxford Tube's No. 390 bus from Oxford to London via Abingdon, Dorchester and Henley.

admission. It is open Easter and April weekends and Tuesdays–Saturdays, May–September, 10.30 a.m.–12.30 p.m. and 2 p.m–6 p.m., plus 2 p.m.–4 p.m. on Sundays and Bank Holiday Mondays.

Refreshments There are refreshments available next to the old Abbey Guest House Museum. Dorchester also has the Fleur de Lys Inn, The George Hotel and shops.

DORCHESTER ABBEY

Route 15   2½ miles
The Letcombes

Outline   Letcombe Regis—Hell Bottom Copse—Letcombe Bassett—Letcombe Brook—Letcombe Regis.

Summary   Both Letcombe Regis and Letcombe Bassett are interesting villages, with thatched cottages. Race horses are the principal livestock in the area and they are evident along this route. The wide, open, fields allow a clear view of the Downs. Along the crest of these hills runs the famous Ridgeway, now a national trail. When you plunge into the trees of Hell Bottom Copse, a false turn could lead you on to it. Sniff the air for the scent of freedom, but reserve the glory of the Ridgeway for another day. It has a rarefied atmosphere which can prove intoxicating. Come to it when you are ready and give it your full attention. Go back to the start along a sheltered path above Letcombe Brook.

Attractions   The deeply incised ravine now occupied by Letcombe Brook is a legacy of the Ice Age. Letcombe Bassett is a spring line village on the narrow belt of greensand at the foot of the chalk scarp of the Downs. Prehistoric men littered the higher ground with their remains, while the impenetrable clay below awaited the heavy iron-tipped ploughs of the Romans and Saxons. Roman coins have been found here, while Alfred the Great was born two miles away at Wantage in 849. The clear spring water fed the watercress that made Letcombe Bassett famous in the streets of London. The beds are now disused, like the osier beds that once provided coppiced willow for basketmaking. Divert into the village to see the springs and think of poor Jude the Obscure. Letcombe Basset was the Cresscombe of Thomas Hardy's last novel. Published in 1895, 'Jude the Obscure' was a tragic work 'for those into whose souls the iron has entered'. Here, at 'Arabella's Cottage', would seem to be the spot where Hardy made the hapless Jude first set eyes on the seductive Arabella as she washed the small intestines of pigs in the stream. Jude had walked from Marygreen, which is Fawley in real life. Hardy's paternal grandmother had spent the first miserable 13 years of her life as an orphan there. Watercress must attract literary minds because Letcombe Bassett Rectory is where Jonathan Swift spent his last summer in England before travelling to Ireland. His 'Verses on Himself' were written here. The church is dedicated to St Michael and has retained a Norman chancel despite being rebuilt in the 19th century. St Andrew's in Letcombe Regis has 14th century stained glass in its east window.

continued on page 68

65

Route 15

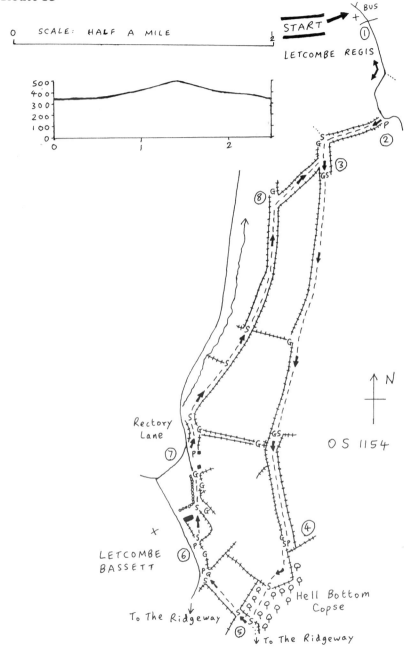

SCALE: HALF A MILE

START

BUS

LETCOMBE REGIS

Rectory Lane

LETCOMBE BASSETT

Hell Bottom Copse

To The Ridgeway

To The Ridgeway

OS 1154

N

Route 15
The Letcombes   2½ miles

START: *St Andrew's church, Letcombe Regis, is at the centre of the village, which is less than two miles south-west of Wantage (G.R. SU 380865).*

ROUTE

1. *Go right to the crossroads and take the road ahead that is signposted 'Village Downs Only'. Follow the road past a variety of houses and cottages until you reach a signposted path on your right where the road bends left (towards the Sparrow Inn).*

2. *Go right along the signposted path. Ignore a stile beside a gate in a corner on your right and follow the enclosed path as it bends left.*

3. *Ignore a path forking right. Go ahead over a stile beside a gate to walk towards the Downs with a fence on your right. Continue over a stile beside a gate ahead to follow an enclosed path to a signpost.*

4. *Turn right over a stile beside a gate and bear left along the signposted path, cutting across the corner of a field to a stile. Cross this to enter woodland and follow the path ahead to another stile. This leads to another path.*

5. *Tempting as the Ridgeway is, turn right for now to follow the path over a stile and beside a fence on your left to the road in Letcombe Bassett. Bear right along it for 100 yards.*

6. *Unless you wish to divert into Hardy's 'Cresscombe', continue by veering right from the road along the signposted path. This goes over a stile, cuts diagonally across a paddock to continue over another stile and follows a wall on your left to a gate. Continue through it to Rectory Lane.*

7. *Bear right away from the road up the signposted path. This crosses three stiles as it follows the edge of the ravine down which Letcombe Brook bubbles on your left. Keep to the sheltering hedge on your right.*

8. *Do not go through a gate ahead. Bear right along the enclosed path to return to your outward route and retrace your steps to the start.*

Public Transport Oxford Minibus operate a service from Wantage to Letcombe Regis (No. 38). There are buses to Wantage from Oxford (Nos. 31 and X31) and Didcot (No. 36).

Refreshments   Letcombe Regis has the Greyhound Inn and the Sparrow Inn. There is a choice of places offering refreshments in Wantage.

LAMBRIDGE WOOD

Henley

Outline   Henley—Lambridge Wood—Lower Assendon—Oxfordshire Way—Henley.

Summary   This is a walk for April or May when the beech woods are carpeted with bluebells. Your path out of Henley climbs to the golf course (where a sign reminds you to beware of the ball rather then the bull!) and into the delightful Lambridge Wood. Descend to cross the A423 at Lower Assendon before joining the Oxfordshire Way on its final stage through parkland down to Henley, where it links with the Thames Path.

Attractions   Henley is a town full of character in a beautiful setting beside the River Thames and at the foot of the Chilterns. No wonder this is where stockbrokers chose to live! If you want to see the Regatta, come in the first week of July. There are plenty of old inns to accommodate you. Hart Street leads uphill from the Thames to the Market Place. One of the gabled Tudor houses opposite the church, where this walk starts, has a plaque to inform us that William Lenthal (1591–1662), Speaker of the Long Parliament (1640–53), was born here. St Mary's church contains the tomb of Lady Elizabeth Periam, a sister of Francis Bacon. Also buried here, in the chancel between her parents, is Mary Blandy. She provided 18th century Henley with a murder story that has been retold to the present day. Mary was the only child of Francis Blandy, a successful solicitor. A pleasant girl, with a trim figure, she was said to be worth a dowry of several thousand pounds and to stand to inherit a fortune. Mary, or Mollie, as she was often called, was still unmarried at the age of 26 because her father had protected her from suitors he considered ineligible. In 1746, however, the Blandy family dined at Paradise House (which stood at the top of Gravel Hill) with General Mark Kerr. There Mary met the general's cousin, Captain the Honourable William Cranstoun. He was small, scarred by smallpox, not considered handsome and 46 years old. He was, however, the son of a Scottish peer, William, fifth Lord Cranstoun. He happened to be this impoverished family's younger son, but Mr Blandy, who was also the town clerk of Henley, found him to be eligible as a prospective son-in-law. The courtship proceeded, aided by the captain being stationed in Henley on recruiting duties (and finding it hard to make ends meet on his pay). General Mark Kerr became aware of the situation, however, and told Blandy that his cousin already had a wife and child in Scotland. Inquiries revealed this to be the case, with the marriage being kept a secret because Anne Murray, whom

continued on page 72

Route 16

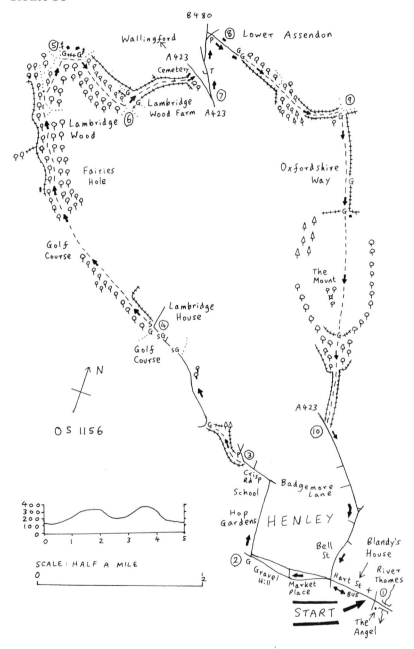

Route 16

Henley   5 miles

START: *Hart Street is easily found, running from Henley Bridge up to the Market Place. Near its foot, opposite St Mary's church, is the Speaker's House, marked by a plaque (G.R. SU 763826).*

ROUTE

1. *With the Speaker's House on your left and the church on your right, go up Hart Street, passing Blandy's House on your right. Continue up Market Place and Gravel Hill.*

2. *Turn right along Hop Gardens. Pass Badgemore C.P. School on your left and turn left up Crisp Road.*

3. *Bear left along a signposted path. Reach a gate and turn right after it along a road. Go ahead over two stiles beside gates across the road.*

4. *When the road bends right, go straight ahead across a stile beside a gate to follow a path across the golf course. Go ahead through the wood, where waymark arrows are painted on trees. Ignore two paths on your right, then fork right to reach the gate of a house at the edge of the wood.*

5. *Turn right to walk with the wood on your right and reach another gate on your left. Bear right along the waymarked bridleway (blue arrow).*

6. *Turn left at a path junction, cross a track, and go down an enclosed path to the A423. Go right for 50 yards, then cross it carefully.*

7. *Go left up the B480 to Lower Assendon. Bear right at a fork.*

8. *Take the waymarked lane on your right. Go through a gate and continue in the same direction along a track past trees. Ignore a path that curves away to your left but bend left soon afterwards to a crosstracks at Henley Park.*

9. *Turn right to follow the waymarked Oxfordshire Way through the park and downhill, passing a mound known as The Mount, on your right. Go through woodland and along an enclosed path to the A423.*

10. *Turn left along the pavement of the A423 into Henley. Pass the shops in Bell Street and turn left down Hart Street back to the start.*

Public Transport You can reach Henley by train. The branch line leaves British Rail's main line at Twyford. Bus services include Oxford Tube's No. 390 from Oxford and London.

he'd wed in Edinburgh in 1744, was a Roman Catholic and a Jacobite. The bridegroom didn't want it to affect his chances of promotion and his wife and daughter hadn't accompanied him to England. Confronted with the truth, Cranstoun told Mary and her parents that the marriage was to be annulled by the Scottish courts. He then gave Mary a brooch of Scottish pebbles as a token of his love. The captain was soon recalled to Scotland, while Mrs Blandy died and Mr Blandy became anxious about his daughter, who still seemed devoted to Cranstoun. News came of difficulties concerning the nullification of the marriage and Blandy forbade his daughter to have anything further to do with the scheming fortune hunter he had encouraged to woo her. Mary was now beyond such reasoning, however. She wrote to Cranstoun, who sent her a packet of white powder, openly to act as a cleaner for the pebbles in the brooch he had given Mary, but secretly as a love potion. It was to be added in small amounts to Mr Blandy's food and would bring about a change of heart! In fact it was arsenic and the deluded girl poisoned her father, who died on 14th August, 1751. A suspicious doctor ordered her arrest, but Mary escaped towards the river and was sheltered at the Angel Inn. Tried at Oxford for murder, Mary protested in vain that she didn't know the powder was arsenic. She was finally hanged on 6th April, 1752. As for Captain Cranstoun, he fled to Flanders and died in agony of arsenic poisoning that December. The Blandy home was in Hart Street and it is now occupied by a dentist. It is an imposing white building on the right as you walk uphill from the river. The Angel stands near Henley Bridge.

Refreshments   There is a choice of places offering refreshments in Henley.

72

PREACHING CROSS, WOODEATON (Route 6)

Appendices

ROUTES IN ORDER OF DIFFICULTY

None of these walks would be strenuous to an experienced walker. The following grading is made in the context of a Family Walks book and is done with the fairly active six or seven year old in mind.

Easy Walks

Route 1—*The Rollright Stones (2¼ miles)*
Route 5—*Rock of Gibraltar (2¾ miles)*
Route 8—*Oxford (4¼ miles)*
Route 9—*Mesopotamia (2¼ miles)*
Route 11—*South of Abingdon (3½ miles)*
Route 12—*Sutton Courtenay (2¼ miles)*
Route 14—*Dorchester (2½ miles)*

Moderately Difficult

Route 2—*West of Charlbury (4½ miles)*
Route 3—*Minister Lovell (3½ miles)*
Route 4—*Blenheim Park (3¼ miles)*
Route 6—*South of Islip (4¾ miles)*
Route 15—*The Letcombes (2½ miles)*

More Strenuous

Route 7—*Happy Valley (2¾ miles)*
Route 10—*Wheatley (3¼ miles)*
Route 13—*Wittenham Clumps (2¼ miles)*
Route 16—*Henley (5 miles)*

PUBLIC TRANSPORT

Oxford is at the centre of a fairly extensive public transport network. The city itself is easy to reach by British Rail or by coach. Local British Rail services go south to Didcot and along the Thames Valley towards London Paddington. Henley has its own branch line from Twyford, with some through trains from Reading. An attractive line goes west to Charlbury (and on to Worcester), while the Cherwell Valley is followed north to Banbury (and on to Birmingham). A line running east to Bicester is useful for reaching Islip. Bus services are split between two main operators, who won't accept each others tickets. Bus Rovers give good value, but plan to use them on only one company's services each day. Timetables are available from Oxford Tourist Information Centre, or contact the individual companies: Oxford Bus Co. tel. 0865 711312 and Oxford Minibus/Oxford Tube tel. 0865 772250. The north of the county is served by Midland Red South tel. 0295 262368. River steamers add an extra dimension to the trip between Oxford and Abingdon. Contact Salter Bros Ltd, tel. 0865 243421.

AN ABINGDON SWAN

75

TOURIST INFORMATION ADDRESSES

Oxford Information Centre, St Aldate's, Oxford, OX1 1DY, tel. 0865 726871. Thames and Chilterns Tourist Board, The Mount House, Church Green Witney, Oxon, OX8 6AZ, tel. 0993 778800.

There are Tourist Information Centres at Abingdon, Banbury, Burford, Chipping Norton, Cropredy, Faringdon, Henley, Oxford, Thame, Wallingford, Witney and Woodstock.

WET WEATHER ALTERNATIVES. Completely or partly under cover.

Oxfordshire is fairly dry by British standards, but if it does rain you could hardly be in a better place for indoor attractions in place of a walk. The following list is not comprehensive and current tourist information should be consulted. It is arranged by its proximity to each walk.

Walk 1	Chipping Norton Museum; Banbury Museum; Broughton Castle; Chastleton House and Bloxham Village Museum.
Walk 2	Charlbury Museum; Combe Mill.
Walk 3	Minster Lovell Hall and Dovecote; Cotswold Wildlife Park; Cogges Manor Farm Museum and Tolsey Museum.
Walk 4	Blenheim Palace; Oxfordshire County Museum and Oxford Bus Museum Trust.
Walk 5	Rousham House.
Walk 6	Studley Priory.
Walks 7, 8 and 9	Oxford United F.C.; Ferry Sports Centre; Temple Cowley Pools; Oxford Ice Rink; Apollo Theatre; Oxford Playhouse; Oxford Story; Ashmolean Museum; Museum of Oxford; University Museum; Pitt Rivers Museum; Bodleian Library; Botanic Gardens; St Michael at the North Gate; Christ Church Cathedral and all of the Oxford Colleges; Museum of the History of Science; Oxfordshire and Buckinghamshire Light Infantry Regimental Museum; British Telecom Museum and Sheldonian Theatre.
Walk 10	Waterperry Gardens and Rycote Chapel.
Walks 11 and 12	Abingdon Museum; Milton Manor House and Didcot Railway Centre and Kingston House.
Walks 13 and 14	Pendon Museum of Landscape and Transport; Wallingford Museum; Dorchester Abbey and Museum and Benson Veteran Cycle Museum.
Walk 15	Vale and Downland Museum Centre; Ardington House; Tom Brown's School Museum, Uffington; Kingstone Lisle Park and Ashdown House.
Walk 16	Stonor Park; Greys Court; Maharajah's Well and Fawley Court Historic House and Museum.

DON'T WANT TO GO HOME!

FAMILY WALKS SERIES

Family Walks in the Lake District. Barry McKay. ISBN 0 907758 40 1.

Family Walks in West Yorkshire. Howard Beck. ISBN 0 907758 43 6.

Family Walks in Three Peaks and Malham. Howard Beck ISBN 0 907758 42 8.

Family Walks in South Yorkshire. Norman Taylor. ISBN 0 907758 25 8.

Family Walks in Cheshire. Chris Buckland. ISBN 0 907758 29 0.

Family Walks in the Staffordshire Peak and Potteries. Les Lumsdon. ISBN 0 907758 34 7.

Family Walks in the White Peak. Norman Taylor. ISBN 0 907758 09 6.

Family Walks in the Dark Peak. Norman Taylor. ISBN 0 907758 16 9.

Family Walks in Snowdonia. Laurence Main. ISBN 0 907758 32 0.

Family Walks in Mid Wales. Laurence Main. ISBN 0 907758 27 4.

Family Walks in South Shropshire. Marian Newton. ISBN 0 907758 30 4.

Family Walks in the Teme Valley. Camilla Harrison. ISBN 0 907758 45 2.

Family Walks in Hereford and Worcester. Gordon Ottewell. ISBN 0 907758 20 7.

Family Walks in the Wye Valley. Heather and Jon Hurley. ISBN 0 907758 26 6.

Family Walks in the Cotswolds. Gordon Ottewell. ISBN 0 907758 15 0.

Family Walks in South Gloucestershire. Gordon Ottewell. ISBN 0 907758 33 9.

Family Walks in Oxfordshire. Laurence Main. ISBN 0 907758 38 X.

Family Walks around Bristol, Bath and the Mendips. Nigel Vile. ISBN 0 907758 19 3.

Family Walks in Wiltshire. Nigel Vile. ISBN 0 907758 21 5.

Family Walks in Berkshire and North Hampshire. Kathy Sharp. ISBN 0 907758 37 1.

Family Walks on Exmoor and the Quantocks. John Caswell. ISBN 0 907758 46 0.

Family Walks in Mendip, Avalon and Sedgemoor. Nigel Vile. ISBN 0 907758 41 X.

Family Walks in North West Kent. Clive Cutter. ISBN 0 907758 36 3.

Ready Spring 1992

Family Walks in the Weald of Kent and Sussex
Family Walks in North Yorkshire
Family Walks around Luton and Dunstable
Family Walks in Northumbria
Family Walks in Nottinghamshire
Family Walks on the Isle of Wight
Family Walks in Clwyd
Family Walks in Dorset
Family Walks in Rossendale, Pendle and Bowland

Other titles under consideration.

The Publishers, D. J. Mitchell and E. G. Power welcome suggestions for further titles in this Series; and will be pleased to consider other manuscripts of Derbyshire and regional interest from new or established authors.
